GCSE

Oxford Literature Companions

The Strange Case of

Dr Jekyll and Mr Hyde

ROBERT LOUIS STEVENSON

WORKBOOK

Notes and activities: Mick Callanan and Adrian Cropper
Series consultant: Peter Buckroyd

OXFORD
UNIVERSITY PRESS

Contents

Introduction	**3**

Plot and Structure	**4**
Plot	4
Structure of the novella	17

Context	**22**
Aspects of the context of Jekyll and Hyde	22
What is context?	24
Stevenson's biography	25
Victorian England	27
The Victorian compromise	30
Religion and science	31
Horror fiction and the gothic	33
Reading today: Rediscovering Jekyll and Hyde	34

Characters	**36**
Dr Henry Jekyll	36
Mr Edward Hyde	42
Mr Gabriel Utterson	48
Dr Hastie Lanyon	50
Mr Richard Enfield	51
Poole	52
Other characters	52

Language	**54**
Use of metaphor	54
Use of simile	55
Personification	56
Dialogue	58
The language of science	61
The language describing Hyde	62
Creating tension and suspense	64
Unfamiliar vocabulary	65

Themes	**68**
Social class in Victorian England	68
Duality in human nature	70
The influence of religion	73
Friendship and loyalty	75
The power of documents	76
Secrets and lies	78
The spirit of place	80

Skills and Practice	**82**
Writing about literary texts in exams	82
Effective revision techniques	82
Plot and structure	83
Character	84
Language	85

Introduction

What are Oxford Literature Companions?

Oxford Literature Companions is a series designed to provide you with comprehensive support for popular set texts. You can use the Companion workbook alongside your novel, using relevant sections during your studies or using the workbook as a whole for revision. The workbook will help you to create your own personalized guide to the text.

What are the main features within this workbook?

Each workbook in the Oxford Literature Companion series follows the same approach and includes the following features:

Activities

Each workbook offers a range of varied and in-depth activities to deepen understanding and encourage close work with the text, covering characters, themes, language and context. The Skills and Practice chapter also offers advice on assessment and includes sample questions and student answers. There are spaces to write your answers throughout the workbook.

Key quotation

Key terms and quotations

Throughout the workbook, key terms are highlighted in the text and explained on the same page. There is also a detailed glossary at the end of the workbook that explains, in the context of the novel, all the relevant literary terms highlighted.

Quotations from the novel appear in blue text throughout this workbook.

Upgrade

As well as providing guidance on key areas of the novel, throughout this workbook you will also find 'Upgrade' features. These are tips to help with your exam preparation and performance.

Progress check

Each chapter of the workbook ends with a 'Progress check'. Through self-assessment, these enable you to establish how confident you feel about what you have been learning and help you to set next steps and targets.

Which edition of the novel has this workbook used?

Quotations have been taken from the Oxford University Press Rollercoasters edition of *The Strange Case of Dr Jekyll and Mr Hyde* (ISBN 978-019-832990-9).

Plot and Structure

The Strange Case of Dr Jekyll and Mr Hyde is a mystery story with elements of both **gothic fiction** and **science fiction**. One of the major achievements of Robert Louis Stevenson's story is that it is a mystery like no other before it. Although short, the story is complex: for instance, the first eight chapters are written from the point of view of Mr Utterson, while Chapters 9 and 10 are first-person accounts by two different characters.

This chapter will help you do the first thing you need to do, which is to remember the **plot**. It will then help you to understand and appreciate its **structure**.

> **gothic fiction** a literary style characterized by tales of horror and the supernatural
>
> **plot** the sequence of events in a narrative
>
> **science fiction** stories that use ideas about scientific discovery to imagine a future that is often frightening
>
> **structure** how a text is organized, overall and in all aspects

Plot

Chapter 1: Story of the Door

In Chapter 1, Stevenson does not allow us to meet his main character, Dr Jekyll; instead, we are introduced to Mr Utterson, who guides the reader through the story for the first eight chapters, and his friend Mr Enfield. Mr Enfield recounts a disturbing story about the violence of Mr Hyde as he trampled a young girl. And, at the end of the chapter, we are left with more questions than answers.

From the start, Stevenson cleverly uses his descriptions of events and characters to set up a series of questions. The reader's curiosity about the answers to these questions drives our engagement with the story and creates the mystery.

Activity 1

Out of the eight questions on pages 5 and 6, four of them remain mysterious at the end of the chapter. The other four are answered during Chapter 1.

a) Identify the questions that Stevenson leaves to be answered in later chapters and circle 'Mystery' beside each one. Then write a sentence for each one, explaining just what makes it mysterious.

b) For each of the rest, circle 'Explained'; then use a quotation from the list below as evidence that we find out the answer in Chapter 1.

The first two have been done for you.

> **Key quotations**
>
> "running as hard as she was able"
>
> "No gentleman but wishes to avoid a scene."
>
> 'the chief jewel of each week'

i. Why don't the two friends want to talk about the 'story of the door' any further?

Mystery   (Explained)

Explanation: The men agree 'a bargain never to refer to this again': they regard it as distasteful to talk about it because the events suggest a gentleman being blackmailed.

ii. Why did Hyde trample the girl calmly for no reason?

(Mystery)   Explained

Explanation: Hyde's unprovoked cruelty towards a small child is shocking and strange; we do not know yet that he is pure evil.

iii. Why was Hyde willing to pay compensation when the girl was not seriously hurt?

Mystery   Explained

Explanation:

- -

- -

iv. Why was someone celebrated as a good man willing to pay for Hyde's wrongdoing?

Mystery   Explained

Explanation:

- -

- -

v. Why does everyone seem to hate Hyde?

Mystery   Explained

Explanation:

- -

- -

vi. Do the men enjoy their Sunday walks?

Mystery   Explained

Explanation:

- -

- -

vii. Why does the girl collide with Hyde?

Mystery   Explained

Explanation:

----

viii. Why does Utterson want to know whether Hyde has a key to the house?

Mystery   Explained

Explanation:

Chapter 2: Search for Mr Hyde

In Chapter 2, the reader meets Hyde for the first time. Mr Utterson, worried about Jekyll's relationship with Hyde, goes looking for this mysterious individual and finds him after waiting at the door. He feels greatly disturbed by meeting him but can't identify exactly why. The encounter causes him to guess the reasons for Jekyll and Hyde's connection and he fears Jekyll must have committed some sin in the past. We also meet two new characters when Utterson speaks to Dr Lanyon and Jekyll's butler, Poole. Dr Lanyon is a friend of both Utterson and Jekyll, although we discover that he no longer speaks to Jekyll.

Activity 2

a) Check Chapter 2 to help you answer the five questions that follow. Find a quotation to support each answer.

i. What is Dr Lanyon's opinion of Jekyll?

----

ii. During his encounter with Utterson, what makes Hyde angry?

----

iii. Where does Hyde go after the encounter?

----

iv. What are Utterson's impressions of Mr Hyde?

----

v. What explanation does Utterson find for Jekyll being blackmailed?

----

b) Now for each one of the five quotations you have written, write a comment on what it tells us about Hyde or Jekyll.

i. --

ii. ---

iii. --

iv. ---

v. --

Chapter 3: Dr Jekyll was Quite at Ease

This chapter is short and simple: Utterson and Jekyll talk about Jekyll's strange will. It is interesting, however, because as a lawyer he feels obliged to agree to help Hyde when Jekyll no longer can. Utterson feels ambivalent (in two minds) about this but, as a professional, he has to put his feelings to one side.

Activity 3

Imagine you are Utterson. On a separate piece of paper, write a short report (marked 'Confidential') explaining what has happened in Chapter 3. The report needs to be written in a neutral tone. It should have four paragraphs, as follows:

a) Express your professional concerns about what has happened so far. For example:

> Dr Jekyll has entrusted me with his will, which is mainly unremarkable. However, I have expressed some concerns to my client.

b) Sum up the mysterious things Jekyll has said about Hyde and the will. For example:

> In answer to my enquiries about the strange terms of the will and its main beneficiary, Dr Jekyll has told me the following...

c) Explain what you have agreed to do. For example:

> Dr Jekyll and I have agreed the following terms...

d) Finish by explaining why you reluctantly agreed to his requests – and your professional concerns about Jekyll's future. For example:

> I have reluctantly agreed to maintain my client's will for these reasons...

Chapter 4: The Carew Murder Case

This is a crucial chapter in the plot: the one and only murder takes place, described in shocking detail; witnessed by a maid who faints at the horror of it. The victim is a well-respected gentleman, Sir Danvers Carew, and there is no doubt about the guilty man – Edward Hyde. Utterson and the police detective hurry to Hyde's home in Soho and find a well-decorated place that Hyde has obviously recently vacated. The police detective remains confident they will catch him as they expect him to visit the bank.

Activity 4

Circle TRUE or FALSE beside each statement. Then write an explanation of your answer, supported by a quotation. The first one has been done for you.

a) The witness struggled to see the events clearly because of the fog.

TRUE   (FALSE)

The fog had cleared and the scene was 'brilliantly lit by the full moon'.

b) The witness recognised the attacker as Mr Hyde.

TRUE   FALSE

----

c) The police were called at 2 a.m. by the witness.

TRUE   FALSE

----

d) The murderer carried away a purse and a gold watch belonging to the victim.

TRUE   FALSE

----

e) The police contact Utterson because he knows where Hyde is.

TRUE   FALSE

----

f) We learn that Jekyll's fortune is worth £250,000.

TRUE   FALSE

----

g) Everyone who had met Hyde agreed on one thing: his family was nowhere to be found.

TRUE   FALSE

You don't get marks for knowing the plot, but it is the basis for all the work that does get marks – such as analysing structure.

Chapter 5: Incident of the Letter

This is a chapter of two halves. In the first, Utterson finds Jekyll in his laboratory. Both he and the lab are in a dreadful state. We don't know it yet, but Jekyll is suffering because his **alter ego**, Edward Hyde, has committed murder. Jekyll gives Utterson a letter from Hyde and promises to have nothing more to do with him.

In the second half of the chapter, Utterson takes the letter to his clerk, Mr Guest, and is told something very interesting about Hyde's autograph…

alter ego second self inside, different from an individual's normal personality

Activity 5

In Chapter 5, everything that Jekyll says and does, and the descriptions of his laboratory, are influenced by the murder Hyde has committed. In each box below, add a quotation to show how Stevenson generates an atmosphere of emotional turmoil and distress. The first one has been done for you.

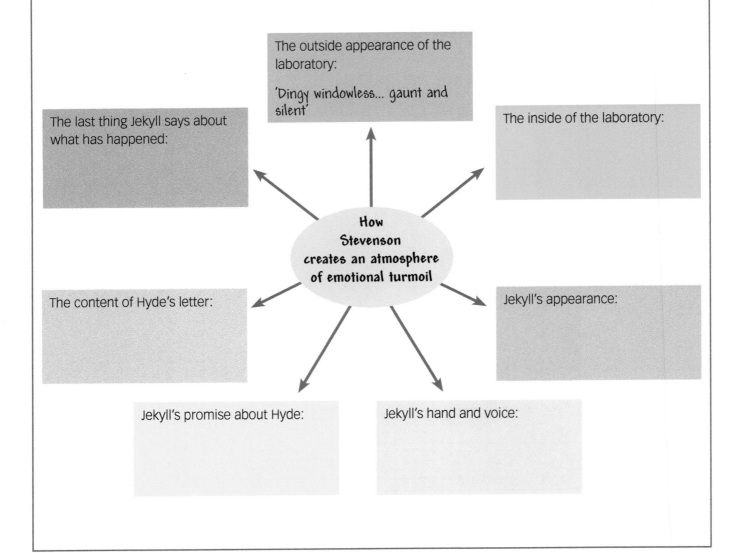

The outside appearance of the laboratory:

'Dingy windowless... gaunt and silent'

The inside of the laboratory:

The last thing Jekyll says about what has happened:

How Stevenson creates an atmosphere of emotional turmoil

The content of Hyde's letter:

Jekyll's appearance:

Jekyll's promise about Hyde:

Jekyll's hand and voice:

Activity 6

At the end of the chapter, Utterson comes to the conclusion that Jekyll has forged his signature **'for a murderer'**, Edward Hyde.

a) Explain why Mr Guest is a particularly appropriate person to check Jekyll and Hyde's handwriting, using a quotation for evidence.

---

b) Explain why Mr Utterson concludes that Jekyll has forged a signature for Hyde.

---

c) Reading between the lines, how does giving the letter to Utterson benefit Jekyll?

Chapter 6: Remarkable Incident of Dr Lanyon

Chapter 6 is again in two parts. At first, Utterson is pleased that the old, sociable Jekyll has re-appeared. But suddenly, matters take a turn for the worse: Jekyll refuses to go out or to accept visitors. This coincides with a terrible shock to Lanyon who refuses even to speak of Jekyll. Soon afterwards, Lanyon dies, leaving Utterson mysterious document to be opened when Jekyll dies – or disappears.

Activity 7

One of Stevenson's main themes is the dual nature of man. This chapter is a typical example of how he divides things in two. List below the signs in Chapter 6 of (a) Jekyll's two months of happiness and (b) Jekyll's unhappy future. You can summarise or, even better, use quotations.

Happy signs	
What has happened to Mr Hyde	
Jekyll's religion	
Jekyll's friendships	
How often Utterson has seen Jekyll in two months	
Jekyll's face	
Jekyll's attitude to Utterson and Lanyon on 8 January	
Where Jekyll was to be seen	

Unhappy signs	
What happens on 12, 14 and 15 January	
What Poole tells him on 14 January	
The change in Lanyon's appearance	
What Lanyon says about Jekyll	
How Lanyon describes the topic of Jekyll	
What happens next to Lanyon	
The letter from Jekyll to Utterson	
The sealed letter from Lanyon to Utterson	
What Poole tells him about Jekyll at the end of the chapter	

Activity 8

The chapter raises more new mysteries as characters continue to be secretive and refuse to discuss matters openly. Find three events or comments that raise Utterson's, and the reader's, curiosity and include a quotation for each.

a) --

----

b) --

----

c) --

Chapter 7: Incident at the Window

In Chapter 7, all of Utterson's concerns are dramatically confirmed by his encounter with Jekyll, who is happy to talk at the window but suddenly shuts it in despair. In many ways, Chapter 7 is a re-run of Chapter 1 but with interesting differences. Their titles are even similar: 'Story of the Door' and 'Incident at the Window'.

Activity 9

Compare the plot of Chapter 7 with that of Chapter 1. How are the events similar and how are they different?

Plot	Chapter 1	Chapter 7
What are Utterson and Enfield doing on Sunday?	Taking a walk together	
Which of them has met Mr Hyde?	Enfield	
Which of them is/are witness(es) to the incident in the chapter?	Enfield	
What is the effect on the witnesses of what they see?	Enfield is horrified and feels loathing for Mr Hyde. He worries for the man who helped him (Jekyll, we later discover).	
How does the chapter end?	They agree not to discuss the matter again.	

Activity 10

a) Another difference between Chapter 1 and Chapter 7 is the way Mr Utterson feels about Jekyll. On a separate piece of paper, write a short paragraph comparing Utterson's views on Jekyll at the time of (i) Chapter 1 and (ii) Chapter 7.

b) Write a second paragraph explaining how, despite the plot developments, Utterson and Enfield have remained the same.

13

Chapter 8: The Last Night

Chapter 8 details one of the most violent and dramatic scenes in *The Strange Case of Dr Jekyll and Mr Hyde*. Poole asks Utterson to come and help his master as he suspects some foul play. Together they break down the door, concerned that Hyde has murdered Jekyll. Stevenson builds up the tension throughout the chapter to create a terrifying climax when Poole and Utterson find Hyde has committed suicide.

Activity 11

Read the list of events from Chapter 8 below and put them in order to demonstrate how the writer creates a rising tide of horror. Then add a quotation for each event that you think demonstrates the tension and drama.

b) Utterson and Poole creep quietly to the cabinet (study) door

a) Hyde is discovered dead

d) The servant does not open the door till Poole says it is him calling

c) Poole visits Utterson late at night, terrified

e) The voice that answers Poole's from behind the door is not his master's

f) Poole tells the lawyer about the letter desperately requesting a particular drug

g) Poole declares his belief that his master has been murdered

h) Poole and Utterson wait for ten minutes and only footsteps can be heard

i) Utterson arms himself with a poker

j) Poole breaks down the door and a screech is heard

1. ☐	6. ☐
2. ☐	7. ☐
3. ☐	8. ☐
4. ☐	9. ☐
5. ☐	10. ☐

Chapter 9: Dr Lanyon's Narrative

Chapter 9 is crucial for the reader. At last we discover the solution to the mystery: Jekyll and Hyde are one person. It is also a tense and exciting part of the **novella** in which we effectively go back in time to hear from Lanyon the cause of his break with Jekyll and his subsequent death.

> **novella** a prose text that is longer than a short story but shorter than a standard novel

The plot of Chapter 9 illustrates the difference between intention and effect. Hyde intends to save his life by having Lanyon get the drug so that he can be restored to the safe form of Dr Jekyll, and Jekyll wants to show him what a great scientist he is. These events happen – but the shock is so great for Dr Lanyon that he dies soon after.

Activity 12

The table below contains a list of Hyde's requests in the letter. Opposite each one, write either what Lanyon thinks of it or the effect it has on him. Find a quotation to support each one. The first has been done for you.

You may wish to use some of the following adjectives: 'surprised', 'confused', 'intrigued', 'afraid', 'terrified'.

Intention. Hyde asks Lanyon to do the following	*Effect*. Lanyon's thoughts or the effect on Lanyon
Save Jekyll's life, honour and reason	Succeeds in the end but at first Lanyon thinks Jekyll has become 'insane'
Go to Jekyll's house and, breaking the lock if necessary, take out the fourth drawer and its contents, including a book	
Let in to his home at midnight a man Lanyon does not know and give him the drawer	
Learn afterwards "if you insist upon an explanation" why this was "of capital importance"	

Activity 13

Chapter 9 is the first time Lanyon sees Hyde – and it is also the last. It is therefore essential that Hyde makes a huge impact. Below write a quotation for each of three aspects of Hyde that make a deep impression on Lanyon.

Behaviour: --

Face: --

Clothing: --

Chapter 10: Henry Jekyll's Full Statement of the Case

The last chapter of the novella takes up almost a quarter of the total – and it is when we finally come to understand precisely what Jekyll does, why he does it and how he feels about it all.

Activity 14

One of the main purposes of Chapter 10 is to answer the reader's remaining questions. In the table below identify which facts are discovered in Chapter 10 by writing a quotation from the chapter that reveals that fact. The first one has been done for you.

Fact	Quotation
Dr Jekyll hides his shameful pleasures from other people	'I... hid them with an almost morbid sense of shame'
Jekyll enjoyed being able to indulge his pleasures as Hyde	
One morning, Jekyll woke up to discover he had turned into Hyde involuntarily	
He felt obliged to choose between being Jekyll or Hyde – and he chose Jekyll	
Jekyll knew that he could never become Hyde again or he would be hanged	
Jekyll behaved much better for two months	
On a lovely day in Regent's Park, Jekyll turned into Hyde involuntarily	
Jekyll could no longer stop himself turning into Hyde so they were both doomed	

Structure of the novella

The structure of *The Strange Case of Dr Jekyll and Mr Hyde* is interesting in a number of ways:

- how Stevenson uses the structure of a novella in an unusual way
- how the author links the plot and the ideas across the ten chapters (as you have already seen in the structural similarities of Chapters 1 and 7)
- how third- and first-person narratives combine for the overall effect.

Stevenson's unusual use of novella structure

Here is a list of five typical features of the structure of a novella, as opposed to a novel:

1. Single plot, with fewer conflicts

2. Single point of view

3. Few characters

4. Lack of elaborate 'back stories' to the characters

5. Focus is personal and emotional rather than on larger social issues.

Activity 15

Stevenson doesn't stick to all the 'rules' of this format. In the table below are five descriptions of *The Strange Case of Dr Jekyll and Mr Hyde*. Fill in the column to the right identifying whether this aspect of *Jekyll and Hyde* fits into the standard novella rules. Then complete the sentences below.

Description of Jekyll and Hyde	Does this follow the novella formula?
There are just four main characters: two doctors, a lawyer and the villain	
The main theme is of one man's self-destruction but big ideas about science and religion etc. are explored too	
Most of the novella is written from a third-person point of view but the last two chapters are testimonies by different characters, typical of 'sensation' fiction, popular from the 1860s onwards	
There are no subplots; even when another character is writing, he is telling us Jekyll's story	
We are given a clear, straightforward summary of how Jekyll's life has led up to his crisis	

Stevenson uses many typical features of a novella in *Jekyll and Hyde,* such as

- -

- -

However, his structure is unusual and interesting, including such features as

- -

- -

The structure of character types for a detective mystery

To understand and analyse structure, you should think of each character as having a role in Stevenson's organization of the plot. Stevenson sets up the plot as a detective mystery in Chapter 1 – a mystery that is finally solved in Chapters 9 and 10.

Activity 16

Fill in the boxes below to show how Stevenson structures the character roles so that each contributes something different to the overall effect.

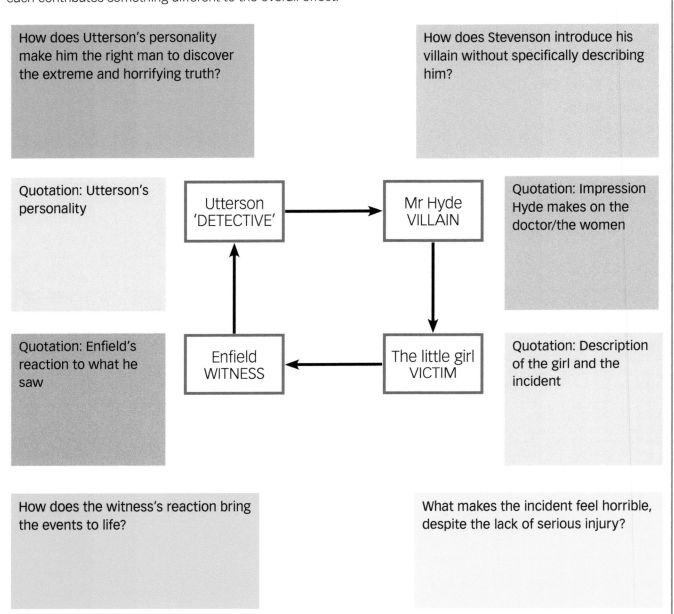

How does Utterson's personality make him the right man to discover the extreme and horrifying truth?

How does Stevenson introduce his villain without specifically describing him?

Quotation: Utterson's personality

Quotation: Impression Hyde makes on the doctor/the women

Utterson 'DETECTIVE'

Mr Hyde VILLAIN

Quotation: Enfield's reaction to what he saw

Enfield WITNESS

The little girl VICTIM

Quotation: Description of the girl and the incident

How does the witness's reaction bring the events to life?

What makes the incident feel horrible, despite the lack of serious injury?

How Stevenson links ideas across chapters: Chapter 7

This chapter is so short – barely two pages – that it is useful to think of it in structural terms as both an addition to Chapter 6 and a preparation for Chapter 8.

Activity 17

Answer the questions below to show how Chapters 6, 7 and 8 link together.

Chapter 6

a) How do events in Chapter 6 lead up to what *will happen* in Chapter 7?
(Clue: Jekyll's relationship with Lanyon)

----

b) In what ways is Chapter 7 the culmination of what *happened* to Utterson in Chapter 6?
(Clue: Lanyon's will and Jekyll's recent behaviour)

Chapter 7 summary

- Utterson and Enfield are glad that Hyde seems to have gone for good
- Utterson is concerned about Jekyll's well-being
- Jekyll looks infinitely sad but is willing to talk
- They see Jekyll's expression suddenly change to one of terror, for no apparent reason
- They leave in silence, apparently unable to help their friend

Chapter 8

c) How does Chapter 8 develop what happens in Chapter 7?

----

d) In what ways does Chapter 7 foreshadow the climax of Chapter 8?

For higher grades, you need to *analyse* the structure of the novella.
But before you can do that, you need to go through two steps:

1. Make sure you understand and remember the main events of the story – its plot.

2. Be able to *describe* the structure of the novel – how it is organised for meaning and effect.

How third- and first-person narratives combine for the overall effect: Chapters 9 and 10

Perhaps the most interesting aspect of Stevenson's use of structure is how and why he uses first-person narration for the last two chapters, after using third-person for the first eight.

First, you need to map the events of Chapters 9 and 10 onto the events we hear about in those first eight chapters so that you can see where they link up. Then, you need to identify how the first-person narratives add to, explain and enrich what the reader already knows.

Activity 18

In the table below, the main event for each of Chapters 1 to 8 is recorded. Find one quotation from Chapter 9 or Chapter 10 about each event and record it in the table. The first one has been done for you.

Main event	Quotation from Chapter 9 or 10
1: Mr Hyde trampled a girl, and an honourable man paid the compensation	'Edward Hyde had to... pay them in a cheque drawn in the name, of Henry Jekyll' (Chapter 10)
2: Utterson finds Hyde and is worried because he is evil and is Jekyll's heir	
3: Jekyll assures Utterson he can be rid of Hyde when he wants	
4: Hyde clubs Sir Danvers Carew to death	
5: Jekyll withdraws from society and Lanyon dies	
6: Jekyll tells Utterson that he has done with Hyde and gives him Hyde's letter	
7: Jekyll shuts his window in despair	
8: Utterson finds Hyde's body and Jekyll's confession	

Activity 19

Now write a paragraph on a separate piece of paper explaining how Chapters 9 and 10 add to the effect of Chapters 1 to 8. For your evidence, find in the table in Activity 18 an example for each of the following:

- the confirmation of an earlier suspicion
- the discovery of something we did not suspect
- the increase of our sympathy for Lanyon
- the increase of our understanding of Dr Jekyll.

Provide a quotation for each point.

Use some of the following sentence starters:

- The plot is made more complex when…
- The reader's response to characters is enhanced during…
- The reading experience is enriched by…
- Satisfying explanations of earlier mysteries are given…

Progress check

Use the chart below to review the skills you have developed in this chapter. For each column, start at the bottom box and work your way up towards the highest level in the top box. Tick the box to show you have achieved that level.

I can sustain a critical response to *Jekyll and Hyde* and interpret the plot and structure convincingly ☐	I can analyse the effects of Stevenson's use of language, structure and form in *Jekyll and Hyde*, using subject terms judiciously ☐
I can develop a coherent response to *Jekyll and Hyde* and explain the plot and structure clearly ☐	I can explain how Stevenson uses language, structure and form to create effects in *Jekyll and Hyde*, using relevant subject terms ☐
I can make some comments on the plot and structure in *Jekyll and Hyde* ☐	I can identify some of Stevenson's methods in *Jekyll and Hyde* and use some subject terms ☐
Personal response	**Language, structure, form**

Context

Aspects of the context of *Jekyll and Hyde*

The **context** in which a text is written, published or read is important because it informs our own interpretation and helps us to understand how the original readers may have responded differently. **The Strange Case of Dr Jekyll and Mr Hyde** explores new ideas in science, religion and psychology, while its style is influenced by gothic fiction. Most importantly, **Victorian society offered a compromise** between a polite outward demeanour and the secret indulgence of less acceptable desires. This is the premise around which *The Strange Case of Dr Jekyll and Mr Hyde* is built.

The following diagram shows the main aspects of context in *Jekyll and Hyde*. Add more explanation and examples to this as you go through this chapter and from any study guides you are using.

colonialism the practice by which an empire rules colonies, to benefit from their resources

context the situation or circumstances in which a text is written, published or read

psychology the scientific study of the mind and how it influences behaviour

Sigmund Freud an influential figure in the early days of the study of the mind; he was particularly interested in deep motivations that we may not even be aware of

Victorian compromise the ability of middle- and upper-class Victorian society to indulge their wilder desires but maintain their outwardly respectable appearance

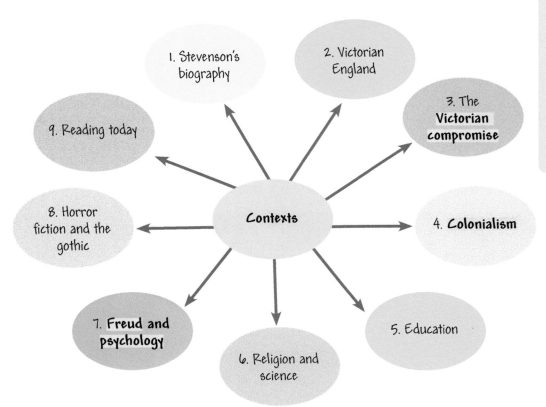

- 1. Stevenson's biography
- 2. Victorian England
- 3. The Victorian compromise
- 4. Colonialism
- 5. Education
- 6. Religion and science
- 7. Freud and psychology
- 8. Horror fiction and the gothic
- 9. Reading today
- Contexts

Activity 1

Add a relevant context title from the diagram above for each of the statements given below, then add another statement related to this context from your own knowledge.

a) Context:_ _

Reading serious books was respectable; going to the music hall was not.

_ _

b) Context:_ _

Jekyll and Hyde was new, combining elements of the gothic with science fiction.

_ _

c) Context:_ _

Victorians had mixed feelings about psychological matters such as sexual orientation but the law of 1885 outlawed sexual contact between men.

_ _

d) Context:_ _

After the famous debate of 1860 between a scientist and an archbishop, most people accepted Darwin's theory of evolution.

_ _

e) Context:_ _

Britain became very prosperous from its empire, but the wealth did not benefit everybody.

_ _

f) Context:_ _

In Victorian society, men of high class were expected to employ domestic staff such as maids and butlers.

_ _

g) Context:_ _

A reader in the 21st century should bear in mind the great shock that the novella gave its first readers.

_ _

h) Context:_ _

Raised as a Christian, Stevenson constantly refers to the Bible, even if he did not believe in God.

_ _

i) Context: _

When Victoria became Queen, 67% of men and 50% of women could read; by the end of the century, over 90% of adults were literate.

_ _

You need to understand how these contexts affect our interpretation of the text. Writing about context should always be related to the text, not a list of historical facts.

What is context?

Which of the following statements are about context? For each pair of statements, one describes context, the other does not but is a related point about the novella. Highlight the context statement. The first one has been done for you.

Context	Statement A	Statement B
Stevenson's biography	Some readers prefer the works of Robert Louis Stevenson to those of Charles Dickens.	Most original readers of Stevenson's work would have read Dickens's books first, as he was the most successful writer of the age.
Victorian England	Jekyll is a wealthy doctor living in London.	For many Londoners, poverty was a way of life at this time.
The Victorian compromise	There are no explicit references to sex or sexual relationships in the novella.	The law on homosexuality was changed in 1885 to outlaw any sexual acts between men.
Colonialism	Stevenson wrote an attack on the poor treatment of Samoa by European empires.	Hyde is portrayed as a savage, animal-like being.
Education	The two females in the novella are both uneducated, minor characters.	In Queen Victoria's Britain, women were less likely to receive an education than men.
Religion and science	Hyde is often referred to as resembling a monkey or ape, e.g. by Poole.	Darwin's theory of evolution changed ideas about humanity in the second half of the 19th century.
Religion and science	Britain was a Christian society and most people knew the Bible well.	Hyde is the most evil person in London and he writes 'blasphemies' on a holy book.
Freud and psychology	The idea of a 'Jekyll and Hyde' personality caught on swiftly from 1886.	Jekyll and Hyde may be seen as opposites but Jekyll is a mixture of good and evil.
Horror fiction and the gothic	Stevenson made *Jekyll and Hyde* frightening by building tension and suspense throughout the novel.	Stevenson intended *Jekyll and Hyde* to be published as a 'Christmas Crawler', a popular type of seasonal horror story.
Reading today	The author uses many literary devices such as **metonymy** to entertain the reader.	Readers today must be careful to separate film adaptations from the original novella.

metonymy the substitution of the name of an attribute for that of the thing meant, for example 'crown' for 'power' or 'authority' in a country

Stevenson's biography

Before the breakthrough success of his novel *Treasure Island* in 1884, Stevenson made a living as a writer. He contributed to the *Pall Mall Gazette*, edited by W.T. Stead, which 'paved the way for the powerful tabloid journalism of the twentieth century'. This journal covered the serious issues of the day and revealed London's hidden side. Its approach could well have influenced Stevenson's ideas and writing. In fact, the real man Stead wrote about in his most famous piece, nicknamed 'The Minotaur of London', is said to have inspired Stevenson's characterisation of Jekyll and Hyde.

Read the extract below about W.T. Stead and complete the activity that follows.

Stead's attack on slum housing in 1883 resulted in new housing legislation being drafted, and in the following year his *The Truth about the Navy* campaign prompted a £3.5 million government handout to update and repair Britain's ageing ships, but his so-called New Journalism was not welcomed by London traditionalists.

Criticism was, in part, motivated by events in the summer of 1885, when Stead shocked the world with one of the most sensational stories ever published in a Victorian newspaper. Acting with the Salvation Army, he uncovered a trade in child prostitution in the London underworld. He was shocked to find that the government knew of the problem but turned a blind eye to protect the trade's wealthy clientele. Enraged, Stead exposed the whole business under the sensational title, *The Maiden Tribute of Modern Babylon*. The story opened respectable society's eyes to the world of London vice – stinking brothels, fiendish procuresses[1], drugs, and padded rooms, where vicious upper-class rakes could enjoy to the full "the exclusive luxury of revelling in the cries of an immature child".

[1] procuress – a woman who gets (or 'procures') something illegal for another; in this case, she procures a child to be abused by a wealthy man

Activity 3

A number of points in the quotation on page 25 have been highlighted. So that you can see how *The Strange Case of Dr Jekyll and Mr Hyde* is typical of the context in which it was written. Match each point with an aspect of the novella by circling the correct answer. The first one has been done for you.

Question	Answer	Answer	Answer
Which area of London do we hear of that had 'slum housing' in 1885?	Gaunt Street	Mayfair	(Soho)
Which 'eminent' friend of Jekyll annoys him because he is a 'traditionalist'?	Utterson	Enfield	Lanyon
Who is willing to 'turn a blind eye' to wrongdoing?	The police detective	The maid who sees the murder	Hyde's housekeeper
Lanyon is a 'respectable' person who has his 'eyes opened' by 'one of the most sensational stories ever'. When?	When Hyde turns into Jekyll	When Jekyll turns into Hyde	When Hyde takes his own life
Which character could be called a 'fiendish procuress'?	The girl whose parents demand compensation	The maid who sees the murder	Hyde's housekeeper
Who is addicted to a 'drug'?	Jekyll	Hyde	Enfield
Jekyll's laboratory is not 'padded' so how does it help him keep his actions secret?	It has no windows and is behind the house	It is in a high tower	It is in an underground vault with one exit
Which 'vicious rake' is unbothered by 'the cries of an immature child'?	Jekyll	Hyde	The surgeon or 'Sawbones'

Victorian England

The Victorian period was one of unprecedented development: the growth of railways, the expansion of factories and the explosion of city populations came together to change the country and, indeed, the world. These changes were powered by burning coal, which in turn caused a horrible change to England's climate: the cities, especially London, were plagued for half of the year by 'pea-soupers' made up of smoke, soot and fog.

The most famous piece of writing about London's infamous fog comes from 1852, when Robert Louis Stevenson was a toddler. In *Bleak House* by Charles Dickens, the author attacks the legal system in England for being corrupt and incredibly slow. He uses fog as an image of how the system stops people seeing clearly.

Read the extract from *Bleak House* below and complete the activities that follow.

Minor sentences like this are used throughout. A minor sentence is one with no main verb so it feels like an unchanging state with no movement.

The description and the fog spread beyond London to the counties around.

> Fog everywhere. Fog up the river, where it flows among green aits and meadows; fog down the river, where it rolls defiled among the tiers of shipping and the waterside pollutions of a great (and dirty) city. Fog on the Essex marshes, fog on the Kentish heights. Fog creeping into the cabooses of collier-brigs; fog lying out on the yards and hovering in the rigging of great ships; fog drooping on the gunwales of barges and small boats. Fog in the eyes and throats of ancient Greenwich pensioners, wheezing by the firesides of their wards; fog in the stem and bowl of the afternoon pipe of the wrathful skipper, down in his close cabin; fog cruelly pinching the toes and fingers of his shivering little 'prentice boy on deck.

Personification: the fog comes to life, hovering purposefully.

Focus on its effect on people is intense and physical.

A powerless, innocent child suffers most in this image.

27

Activity 4

Response to Dickens's fog: make your response to context analytical by paying close attention to details. Use the annotations to the extract on page 27 to help you fill in the gaps in the analysis and complete the summary sentence below.

> Dickens uses .... sentences: 'Fog on the Essex marshes, fog on the Kentish heights.' Because there is no main ...., it feels as if this fog is a fixed state with no chance of movement. The description and the fog stretch away in the mind's eye of the .... past the ships to the counties around London, making it inescapable. Dickens uses .... a number of times: first, the fog comes to life, 'creeping', 'lying' and 'drooping'. Then the focus of the passage shifts to the fog's effect on people ('in the eyes and throats of ancient Greenwich pensioners', etc.).

As a result, the overall impression of Victorian London is _

_ _

_ _

Activity 5

a) Now analyse how Stevenson uses the description of this context differently, in Chapter 4, to create a different mood. First fill in the annotation boxes to help you focus on Stevenson's precise techniques. Use the Dickens example on page 27 as a model.

1

2

5

7

3

4

6

> It was by this time about nine in the morning, and the first fog of the season. A great chocolate-coloured pall lowered over heaven, but the wind was continually charging and routing these embattled vapours; so that as the cab crawled from street to street, Mr Utterson beheld a marvellous number of degrees and hues of twilight; for here it would be dark like the back-end of evening; and there would be a glow of a rich, lurid brown, like the light of some strange conflagration; and here, for a moment, the fog would be quite broken up, and a haggard shaft of daylight would glance in between the swirling wreaths. The dismal quarter of Soho seen under these changing glimpses, with its muddy ways, and slatternly passengers, and its lamps, which had never been extinguished or had been kindled afresh to combat this mournful reinvasion of darkness, seemed, in the lawyer's eyes, like a district of some city in a nightmare. The thoughts of his mind, besides, were of the gloomiest dye;

b) Now answer the following questions about each of the annotations.

i What are the connotations of 'chocolate' and 'heaven'?

----

ii Personification: how does it make us feel?

----

iii How do the different shades of the fog add to the mood?

----

iv A second personification: what different effect does it have?

----

v The first people in the passage: how do we feel about them?

----

vi What is the effect of this military image?

----

vii The fog has got into Utterson's head – in what way?

Activity 6

On a separate piece of paper, write an analysis of how Stevenson uses the context of London fog to create atmosphere. Use the analysis of the Dickens extract in Activity 4 on page 28 as your model. In the same way, link up different points from your annotations to complete the analysis. The first few sentences have been done for you.

> Stevenson uses many different images of fog to create an unsettling, gloomy atmosphere. He ironically combines 'chocolate-coloured', which should be sweet, with 'pall', which suggests a shroud for a dead body. The fog lowers over 'heaven', putting a barrier between us and it; we may feel closer to Hyde's hell in this weather. Metaphorically, the wind is a brave soldier...

The Victorian compromise

Jekyll has two main motives for what he does: one is scientific curiosity, the other is 'undignified pleasures' that the respectable doctor feels ashamed to enjoy because of his position in society. He is torn between his desire to maintain his respectability and enjoy his 'darker' side.

Activity 7

Read the extract from Chapter 10 below. Highlight the words and phrases that show the following (use different colours for each):

- Jekyll's position in society
- why Jekyll wants his desires to be hidden
- that Jekyll's desires could have been seen as acceptable.

> And indeed the worst of my faults was a certain impatient gaiety of disposition, such as has made the happiness of many, but such as I found it hard to reconcile with my imperious desire to carry my head high, and wear a more than commonly grave countenance before the public. Hence it came about that I concealed my pleasures; and that when I reached years of reflection, and began to look round me and take stock of my progress and position in the world, I stood already committed to a profound duplicity of life. Many a man would have even blazoned such irregularities as I was guilty of; but from the high views that I had set before me, I regarded and hid them with an almost morbid sense of shame. It was thus rather the exacting nature of my aspirations than any particular degradation in my faults, that made me what I was and, with even a deeper trench than in the majority of men, severed in me those provinces of good and ill which divide and compound man's dual nature.
> *(Chapter 10)*

It's never made clear what sort of pleasures Jekyll wishes to indulge in as Hyde. Some possibilities are that he is a homosexual, he is addicted to drugs or alcohol, he attends the music hall or freak shows, or he uses prostitutes.

Activity 8

Write down two reasons why you think Stevenson chose not to include this detail in the novella.

1. --

----

2. --

Religion and science

The most significant scientific theory of the 19th century was the theory of evolution. Charles Darwin proposed that man and the great apes had a common ancestor from which they had evolved. This shook the foundations of Christianity, which was a powerful force in upholding the morals of the time. A great fear for many Victorians was 'atavism' – the possibility that evolution could be reversed and a human could be a throwback to that earlier animal state. One strong interpretation of Edward Hyde is that he is a kind of ape, imagined by Stevenson in the light of Darwin's theory of evolution. The activities below will help you decide to what extent you are convinced by this idea.

Activity 9

Read the extract below from Charles Darwin's *The Descent of Man*. In it, Darwin describes the major differences between human beings and apes.

> There can be no doubt that the difference between the mind of the lowest man and that of the highest animal is immense. An anthropomorphous ape, if he could take a dispassionate view of his own case, would admit that though he could form an artful plan to plunder a garden—though he could use stones for fighting or for breaking open nuts, yet that the thought of fashioning a stone into a tool was quite beyond his scope. Still less, as he would admit, could he follow out a train of metaphysical reasoning, or solve a mathematical problem, or reflect on God, or admire a grand natural scene. Some apes, however… might insist that they were ready to aid their fellow-apes of the same troop in many ways, to risk their lives for them, and to take charge of their orphans; but they would be forced to acknowledge that disinterested love for all living creatures, the most noble attribute of man, was quite beyond their comprehension.

Match each description of human beings and apes from the extract on page 31 with one quotation from the novella, below. Then write in the table whether each applies to Jekyll or Hyde or both.

Darwin quotation	Jekyll and Hyde quotation	Jekyll or Hyde or both
'the difference between the mind of the lowest man and that of the highest animal is immense'	'My two natures had memory in common, but all other faculties were most unequally shared between them.' (Chapter 10)	
'take a dispassionate view of his own case'	'There comes an end to all things … and this brief condescension to my evil finally destroyed the balance of my soul.' (Chapter 10)	
'form an artful plan'	'[…] a second or two to mix and swallow the draught … and whatever he had done, Edward Hyde would pass away like the stain of breath upon a mirror' (Chapter 10)	
'use stones or what is to hand for fighting'	'[…] broke out of all bounds and clubbed him to the earth. And next moment, with ape-like fury… hailing down a storm of blows' (Chapter 4)	
'follow out a train of metaphysical reasoning'	'Had I approached my discovery in a more noble spirit… all must have been otherwise, and… I had come forth an angel instead of a fiend.' (Chapter 10)	
'reflect on God'	'I was driven to reflect deeply… on that hard law of life, which lies at the root of religion… both sides of me were in dead earnest' (Chapter 10)	
'admire a grand natural scene'	'[…] a fine, clear, January day… the Regent's park was full of winter chirruppings and sweet with Spring odours.' (Chapter 10)	
'ready to aid their fellow-apes'	'[…] Hyde was indifferent to Jekyll, or but remembered him as the mountain bandit remembers the cavern in which he conceals himself' (Chapter 10)	
'disinterested love for all living creatures'	'I laboured… at the furtherance of knowledge or the relief of sorrow and suffering.' (Chapter 10)	

Activity 10

Using the evidence that you have created in the table on page 32, write an argument for or against the idea that Hyde represents an ape, as imagined by Darwin. The opening sentence has been written for you.

On the basis of how Darwin describes the differences between humans and apes, I would say that Hyde does/ does not represent an ape. One example is

-----

Horror fiction and the gothic

At the same time as he was completing *Jekyll and Hyde*, Stevenson wrote a gothic short story called *Olalla*. Thinking about it will help you to appreciate the ways in which *Jekyll and Hyde* is also gothic – and the ways in which the novella goes beyond its conventions to become something new and unique.

Activity 11

Read the summary of *Olalla* below and an extract from it, then complete the table to show how both *Olalla* and *Jekyll and Hyde* have many gothic elements. To fill in the *Olalla* column, write one piece of evidence from the summary or extract. To fill in the *Jekyll and Hyde* column, decide whether the gothic element applies or not. If it does, write in an example. If it does not, explain why. The first one has been done for you.

Summary of *Olalla*

Earlier in the 19th century, an English soldier travels to a far-flung part of Spain to recuperate from his war wounds. He stays at a crumbling and labyrinthine mansion, with pictures of wicked but mesmerising ancestors lining the walls. Its inhabitants are equally strange: the mother barely moves, while her son is a simpleton. When the soldier cuts himself, the mother bites his finger, trying to replace her own weakened blood with his. Her daughter, however, is innocent and strikingly beautiful – and the soldier falls deeply in love. She returns his feelings but rejects his offer of marriage because she is determined never to pass on the hereditary flaw that has afflicted her family. He leaves her praying at a roadside crucifix.

Extract from *Olalla*

❝ [The mother] looked up sleepily and asked me what it was, and with the very words I thought she drew in her breath with a widening of the nostrils and seemed to come suddenly and fully alive.

'I have cut myself,' I said, 'and rather badly. See!' And I held out my two hands from which the blood was oozing and dripping.

Her great eyes opened wide, the pupils shrank into points; a veil seemed to fall from her face, and leave it sharply expressive and yet inscrutable. And as I still stood, marvelling a little at her disturbance, she came swiftly up to me, and stooped and caught me by the hand; and the next moment my hand was at her mouth, and she had bitten me to the bone. The pang of the bite, the sudden spurting of blood, and the monstrous horror of the act, flashed through me all in one, and I beat her back… ❞

Olalla	Gothic elements	Jekyll and Hyde
Olalla is set earlier on in the 19ᵗʰ century	Period: the past	No – *Jekyll and Hyde* is set at the time Stevenson wrote it
	Setting: exotic, often Southern Europe	
	Landscape: isolated, extreme	
	Ancestors are a great influence, often seen in portraits	
	Hereditary curse	
	Isolated protagonist	
	Sinister villain	
	Horror	
	Dread	
	Mystery	
	The supernatural	

Reading today: Rediscovering *Jekyll and Hyde*

The single most important thing about context that a student needs to remember is this: the original readers of *Jekyll and Hyde* had never heard of the characters and didn't know that Jekyll and Hyde were one and the same person! Nowadays, we are very familiar – maybe too familiar – with them. There have been dozens of adaptations for TV and film, and the expression 'Jekyll and Hyde personality' has come to mean 'a person who can switch from nice to nasty in a moment'.

Activity 12

This activity will help you to imagine how an original reader might have responded. Below are three summaries of the plot that you might find on a website about the novella, followed by a list of six reactions that readers in 1886 might have had to the facts they reveal. For each summary, match two emotions and thoughts that a Victorian reader might have had from the list on the right.

Friends of the celebrated Dr Jekyll are worried: why has he promised to leave his fortune to the devilish Hyde *(Chapter 2)* if he dies – or disappears? Even his closest friends can't imagine just how dreadful the truth is…

A little girl is trampled in the street. A kindly gentleman is clubbed to death. Both must be the work of Mr Hyde, who fills anyone he meets with loathing. But why is the successful and popular Dr Jekyll willing to protect this monster?

Wealth, reputation, friendship: Dr Jekyll has it all. But, tired of a dry, dusty life of being good, he is willing to risk everything for the other side of life. What happens behind the closed door of Jekyll's laboratory? And can his true friend Utterson help before Jekyll destroys himself?

'Curiosity: why would a respectable man fear 'disappearing'?

Disgust: this apparently perfectly good man has brought on his own destruction by giving in to temptations that any educated, Christian man ought to be able to resist.

Terror: if he is willing to kill this 'kindly gentleman' for seemingly nothing, what will Hyde stop at?

Concern: why would he leave his fortune to this 'devilish' person? Is he being blackmailed for the errors of his youth?

Hope: this lawyer is a gentleman who could save the day.

Suspicion: if this fellow Jekyll is standing by a murderer, he must have something very serious to hide – that Hyde must know of!

Progress check

Use the chart below to review the skills you have developed in this chapter. For each column, start at the bottom box and work your way up towards the highest level in the top box. Tick the box to show you have achieved that level.

Textual references	Text and context	Technical accuracy
I can use well-integrated textual references from *Jekyll and Hyde* to support my interpretation	I can show a perceptive understanding of how *Jekyll and Hyde* is shaped by its context	I use a wide range of vocabulary and can spell and punctuate consistently accurately
I can use quotations and other textual references from *Jekyll and Hyde* to support my explanation	I understand the context of *Jekyll and Hyde* and can make connections between the text and its context	I use a range of vocabulary and can spell and punctuate, mostly accurately
I can make references to some details from *Jekyll and Hyde*	I am aware of the context in which *Jekyll and Hyde* was written	I use a simple range of vocabulary and spell and punctuate with some accuracy

Characters

Dr Henry Jekyll

One of the 'two' **eponymous protagonists**, Dr Henry Jekyll is a respected gentleman in his fifties who becomes the victim of his own dual personality and skill as a scientist. Throughout the narrative the reader is introduced to the wealthy Dr Jekyll through his friends' worries, concern and fear for his sanity and safety. The character is essentially selfish as he transforms himself in order to enjoy pleasures denied 'Dr Jekyll'. However, he is ultimately able to feel 'the horror of being Hyde' *(Chapter 10)* and it is perhaps this that leads to his redemption, removing both of his selves from the world.

> **eponymous** refers to the character's name forming part of the title of the novel
>
> **protagonist** a main character

Key quotations

'And yet when I looked upon that ugly idol in the glass, I was conscious of no repugnance, rather of a leap of welcome.' *(Chapter 10)*

'He had now seen the full deformity of that creature that shared with him some of the phenomena of consciousness, and was co-heir with him to death:' *(Chapter 10)*

Upgrade

When writing about the character-construct Dr Jekyll, it is important to remember he is always consciously acting as 'himself' of his own volition – even in the guise of Mr Hyde. There is only one character – albeit with two differing traits and extremes of personality and behaviour.

Activity 1

Until the final chapter (written from the perspective of Dr Jekyll), the reader mainly learns about Dr Jekyll through the comments of the other characters and through his responses in conversation.

Look at the following list, which contains quotations about/from Dr Jekyll in the first nine chapters.

Sort the quotations into the correct chronological order by noting which chapter the quotation is from, then add who said each quotation.

Quotation	Chapter	Who said it?
'[...] and the person that drew the cheque is the very pink of proprieties, celebrated too'		
'[...] a large, well-made, smooth-faced man of fifty'		
"If I am the chief of sinners, I am the chief of sufferers also."		
"Your master, Poole, is plainly seized with one of those maladies that both torture and deform the sufferer"		
"[...] do you think I do not know my master after twenty years?"		
"He began to go wrong, wrong in mind"		
"Think of me at this hour, in a strange place, labouring under a blackness of distress that no fancy can exaggerate"		
"[...] we heard him cry out upon the name of God; and *who's* in there instead of him"		
"Such unscientific balderdash"		
'What he told me in the next hour, I cannot bring my mind to set on paper.'		
'[...] grew pale to the very lips, and there came a blackness about his eyes.'		
'[...] and there, close up to the warmth, sat Dr Jekyll, looking deadly sick.'		
'"I do not blame our old friend," Jekyll wrote, "but I share his view that we must never meet."'		
"He was wild when he was young; a long while ago to be sure"		

Activity 2

Focus on the second and third chapters for this activity. The character of Dr Jekyll is portrayed through the comments of Dr Lanyon and the thoughts of Mr Utterson in Chapter 2. In Chapter 3 the character is directly presented in conversation with Mr Utterson.

a) Find evidence from these chapters that suggests that Stevenson is leading the reader to pity and/or to suspect Jekyll.

----

b) What do you think the writer wants the reader to think and feel about Dr Jekyll by the end of Chapter 3? Write a paragraph to discuss the portrayal of the character in this part of the story. Use some short integrated quotations you have found in your answer to a) to support the points you make.

You may wish to include some of the following points to help develop your thinking and argument.

Chapter 2: Search for Mr Hyde

- The role of the will
- The attitude of Dr Lanyon
- Utterson's fears for the safety of Dr Jekyll

Chapter 3: Dr Jekyll was Quite at Ease

- The description of their friendship
- Dr Jekyll's attitude towards their mutual friend, Dr Lanyon
- His reluctance to discuss Mr Hyde

In the final chapter, Dr Jekyll is given a voice through the device of the testimonial read by Mr Utterson after the revelations of 'Dr Lanyon's Narrative'. From Lanyon's written account, the reader is at this point aware of the eyewitness account of Hyde's physical transformation into Jekyll after the ministering of the chemicals. The writer allows Dr Jekyll to analyse his own character, looking for the traits that led him to seek other ways to fulfil the desires he was unable to access as 'himself'. In the first page of the chapter he argues his reasoning for seeking to release his other self.

Activity 3

In the table below there is a mixture of quotations and explanations from the opening line of Chapter 10 to the sentence ending **'or the relief of sorrow and suffering'**. Where there is a quotation, try to explain its significance. Where there is an explanation, find an appropriate quotation. The first is completed for you.

Quotation	Significance
'I was born in the year 18— to a large fortune'	His family were wealthy – he was privileged at a time when most people were poor and had few prospects
	Born with good health and intelligence
'[...] inclined by nature to industry'	
	Betrays a need to be recognized in higher social circles
'[...] with every guarantee of an honourable and distinguished future.'	
	He sometimes desired to act in a way that would be seen as ungentlemanly by 'polite society'
'[...] my imperious desire to carry my head high'	On reaching middle and later life
'[...] I stood already committed to a profound duplicity of life.'	
	His character was 'true' and 'honest' – whichever side was dominant

Activity 4

Think about what has been learned from Dr Jekyll's state of mind from the last activity. Both Mr Utterson and the reader are aware that when this was written, Jekyll (in the guise of Mr Hyde) was already guilty of outrageously aggressive acts and the murder of Sir Danvers Carew.

a) How does this introduction to his confession justify his motives or explain his actions?

----

b) Jekyll gives details about his privileged start in life. What effect does this have on the reader's opinion of him?

----

c) Was he acting purely out of his own selfish desires or to further scientific knowledge when he learned how to release Mr Hyde? Find evidence to support your opinion.

Later in the final chapter, Stevenson includes a paragraph where Dr Jekyll describes how he chose to ignore the demands of his alter ego and forcibly denied himself the pleasures he knew he could enjoy. However, he was unable to resist for more than two months. When he finally succumbed to the compulsion, it was the last time that he had any semblance of control. This is the significant moment that effectively kills the personality embodied by the recognisable physical form of Dr Jekyll. The writer skilfully presents the grip of the addiction that controls Dr Jekyll through the character's tone when describing the dual nature of his mind.

Activity 5

Reread the paragraph below and note the highlighted sections. Answer the questions below, which are designed to explore your understanding of the passage.

> Yes, I preferred the elderly and discontented doctor, surrounded by friends and cherishing honest hopes; and bade a resolute farewell to the liberty, the comparative youth, the light step, leaping pulses and secret pleasures, that I had enjoyed in the disguise of Hyde. I made this choice perhaps with some unconscious reservation, for I neither gave up the house in Soho, nor destroyed the clothes of Edward Hyde, which still lay ready in my cabinet. For two months, however, I was true to my determination; for two months, I led a life of such severity as I had never before attained to, and enjoyed the compensations of an approving conscience. But time began at last to obliterate the freshness of my alarm; the praises of conscience began to grow into a thing of course; I began to be tortured with throes and longings, as of Hyde struggling after freedom; and at last, in an hour of moral weakness, I once again compounded and swallowed the transforming draught. *(Chapter 10)*

a) The two highlighted sections are in different colours because there is a clear **juxtaposition**. What is being juxtaposed?

----

b) Select some words and phrases that betray Jekyll's preferences and explain how they convey this to the reader.

----

c) Why does he describe his **'determination'** as having led to **'a life of such severity'**?

----

d) How does the description of his final decline emphasise the victory of his addiction? Select some words and phrases to support your conclusion.

----

juxtaposition one thing put next to another for contrast

Mr Edward Hyde

The second of the 'two' eponymous protagonists, Hyde is the dominant presence in the novella because of the horror he strikes into the hearts of others and his disregard for human life. He is mainly depicted as a destructive force, both of others and ultimately Jekyll himself. Jekyll is able to exercise his 'irregularities' *(Chapter 10)* through Hyde without losing public face and respect. He is consistently portrayed as an evil force and as embodying the dark side of human nature. Jekyll loses control of his alter ego through the intense and strengthening will of Hyde. He chooses to die, destroying the entity known as Hyde while he still can.

Activity 6

a) The following quotations describe Edward Hyde. Note down who said each of them.

"There is something wrong with his appearance; something displeasing, something downright detestable." *(Chapter 1)*

"God bless me, the man seems hardly human! Something troglodytic, shall we say?" *(Chapter 2)*

"Particularly small and particularly wicked-looking, is what the maid calls him" *(Chapter 4)*

'Much of his past was unearthed, indeed, and all disreputable: tales came out of the man's cruelty, at once so callous and violent, of his vile life, of his strange associates' *(Chapter 6)*

'I knew myself, at the first breath of this new life, to be more wicked, tenfold more wicked, sold a slave to my original evil' *(Chapter 10)*

'[...] Hyde was indifferent to Jekyll' *(Chapter 10)*

'And yet when I looked upon that ugly idol in the glass, I was conscious of no repugnance, rather of a leap of welcome.' *(Chapter 10)*

'He had now seen the full deformity of that creature that shared with him some of the phenomena of consciousness, and was co-heir with him to death.' *(Chapter 10)*

----

b) Now highlight all the adjectives in the quotations above. Create a spider diagram for Edward Hyde on a separate piece of paper and add these adjectives to it, along with any more you can find.

Activity 7

In the first three chapters the reader is introduced to Edward Hyde from a range of perspectives. We hear Enfield's description of the man who trampled over the young girl, Utterson's thoughts linked to Jekyll's will, Utterson's actual meeting with Hyde and Dr Jekyll's explanation and request. Look at the following table, which contains references to Hyde. The picture builds with the chronological references. Explain what you feel the writer wants the reader to feel about the character at each point. The first is suggested as an example.

Quotation	Chapter and perspective	What it shows/suggests
'[…] the man trampled calmly over the child's body and left her screaming'	1 (Enfield)	This initial description immediately portrays the kind of behaviour that breaks the social norm/rule that adults should always protect children from harm
'[…] I saw that Sawbones turn sick and white with the desire to kill him.'	1 (Enfield)	
'[…] out of the shifting, insubstantial mists that had so long baffled his eye, there leaped up the sudden, definite presentment of a fiend.'	2 (Utterson)	
'Yes,' returned Mr Hyde, 'it is as well we have met; and à propos, you should have my address.'	2 (Utterson)	
'But tonight there was a shudder in his blood; the face of Hyde sat heavy on his memory;'	2 (Utterson)	
'[…] if this Hyde suspects the existence of the will, he may grow impatient to inherit.'	2 (Utterson)	
'I only ask for justice; I only ask you to help him for my sake, when I am no longer here.'	3 (Jekyll)	

Activity 8

Throughout the text Edward Hyde is described as inhuman, animal-like and possessed with a hateful force that makes all whom he meets recoil from his presence. A selection of descriptions of Hyde's unusual behaviour from across the whole novella is given below, along with explanations of their significance. However, both the references and the explanations are listed out of chronological order.

Draw lines between the matching references and explanations – you will develop your learning and use the information in Activity 9.

Quotation	Explanation/analysis
'[...] he broke out in a great flame of anger, stamping with his foot, brandishing the cane' *(Chapter 4)*	Utterson's first meeting with Hyde 'in person' suggesting aspects of animal behaviour
'I gnashed my teeth upon him with a gust of devilish fury' *(Chapter 10)*	Utterson's account of Poole attacking the study door with an axe. The reaction of the persona of Hyde is likened to that of an animal.
'The other snarled aloud into a savage laugh' *(Chapter 2)*	The maid's eye witness account of the murder of Sir Danvers Carew. The description focuses on uncontrollable and unpredictable violence.
'[...] I could hear his teeth grate with the convulsive action of his jaws' *(Chapter 10)*	Dr Lanyon's account of Hyde's actions as he arrived at his residence 'representing' Jekyll in order to pick up the drawer of chemicals
'[...] there was something abnormal and misbegotten in the very essence of the creature that now faced me' *(Chapter 9)*	Dr Lanyon describing Hyde's appearance when he is becoming increasingly desperate for his chemicals
"[...] when that masked thing like a monkey jumped from among the chemicals" *(Chapter 8)*	Poole's account of seeing Hyde rush towards Jekyll's cabinet (study) when discovered
"It wasn't like a man, it was like some damned Juggernaut." *(Chapter 1)*	Dr Jekyll's account of how he behaved as Hyde, intent on reaching Dr Lanyon's residence
'A dismal screech, as of mere animal terror, rang from the cabinet.' *(Chapter 8)*	Hyde is objectified, described as thoughtlessly acting like a machine – with no empathy

Activity 9

The references to beast-like behaviour you have read in the table in Activity 8 represent the gradual weakening of Dr Jekyll's humanity in his guise as Edward Hyde. Use the information gathered from Activity 7 and other impressions you have gathered from your reading to help you complete the following activity.

On a separate piece of paper, write a paragraph of approximately 150 words discussing the ways that Robert Louis Stevenson presents Hyde's lack of humanity.

The character of Edward Hyde is not always presented as a monster. Aside from physical descriptions and the intense reactions of all who encounter him for the first time, there is one aspect of Hyde that seems remarkably 'normal' – his speech. Remember, Hyde is Jekyll and so when he is in conversation with others, he speaks with the same level of language as the educated Jekyll.

Activity 10

Look at the following points in the narrative where Hyde speaks to others. Write down beneath them some examples of the polite words and phrases used by a man depicted as a wild and uncontrollable creature for the majority of the novella.

Chapter 1	Enfield recounts the incident where he confronted Hyde with a group of people after Hyde had trampled over the young girl.
Chapter 2	Utterson speaks to Hyde after waiting outside the door in the alley until he returns at night (i.e. before the **'savage laugh'** and Hyde's exit)
Chapter 9	Hyde's reaction to Dr Lanyon when he is asked to make his acquaintance more politely
Chapter 9	Hyde's warning to Dr Lanyon that he should leave the room (before he takes the chemicals needed to transform)

The effect of the sight of Hyde is described from the perspective of all the characters who see him in the novella. One of the most interesting is the account of Dr Lanyon in Chapter 9. He describes the visit of Hyde on the night that he ultimately witnesses him transforming physically back into Dr Jekyll. The 'particulars' mentioned at the beginning of the extract below refer to the fact that Hyde had entered the house quickly and Lanyon thought the presence of an approaching policeman with a bright lamp (called a 'bull's eye' in the novella) had hurried his 'guest'.

These particulars struck me, I confess, disagreeably; and as I followed him into the bright light of the consulting room, I kept my hand ready on my weapon. Here, at last, I had a chance of clearly seeing him. I had never set eyes on him before, so much was certain. He was small, as I have said; I was struck besides with the shocking expression of his face, with his remarkable combination of great muscular activity and great apparent debility of constitution, and – last but not least – with the odd, subjective disturbance caused by his neighbourhood[1]. This bore some resemblance to incipient rigor[2], and was accompanied by a marked sinking of the pulse. At the time, I set it down to some idiosyncratic, personal distaste, and merely wondered at the acuteness of the symptoms; but I have since had reason to believe the cause to lie much deeper in the nature of man, and to turn on some nobler hinge than the principle of hatred.

This person (who had thus, from the first moment of his entrance, struck in me what I can only describe as a disgustful curiosity) was dressed in a fashion that would have made an ordinary person laughable: his clothes, that is to say, although they were of rich and sober fabric, were enormously too large for him in every measurement – the trousers hanging on his legs and rolled up to keep them from the ground, the waist of the coat below his haunches, and the collar sprawling wide upon his shoulders. Strange to relate, this ludicrous accoutrement was far from moving me to laughter. Rather, as there was something abnormal and misbegotten in the very essence of the creature that now faced me – something seizing, surprising and revolting – this fresh disparity seemed but to fit in with and to reinforce it; so that to my interest in the man's nature and character, there was added a curiosity as to his origin, his life, his fortune and status in the world.
(Chapter 9)

[1]neighbourhood – Dr Lanyon is referring to the effect of the proximity of Hyde (how close he was to Lanyon)

[2]incipient rigor – Dr Lanyon is describing the onset (beginning) of a physical reaction to Hyde that makes him stiffen

Activity 11

a) Highlight the extract on page 46 to show:

    i. direct descriptions of Hyde's appearance

    ii. the physical and emotional reaction of Dr Lanyon.

b) Now write a paragraph to explore how Dr Lanyon's perception of and reaction to Hyde presents Hyde as an evil being. Use the quotations you picked out in a). Write your answer on a separate piece of paper.

Activity 12

The battle between 'good' and 'evil' is fundamental in religious thinking. All religions embody the ultimate power of evil in a particular individual (e.g. the fallen angel, the devil or Satan in Christianity). To the **Calvinists** it is when evil takes on a human aspect that it becomes most terrifying.

In the following table there are a number of direct references to evil related to Edward Hyde's behaviour or appearance. In the table there is a mixture of quotations and explanations. Where there is a quotation, try to explain its significance. Where there is an explanation, find an appropriate quotation. The first is completed for you.

Chapter	Quotation	Explanation
1	"[...] it was hellish to see"	The use of the adjective 'hellish' makes the act of Hyde even more callous and cruel and highlights his lack of empathy
2	"[...] but carrying it off, sir, really like Satan."	
2		Utterson explains very strongly just how harmful a 'friend' Hyde could be for Jekyll after meeting Hyde in person
8	"Evil, I fear, founded – evil was sure to come – of that connection."	
10		Jekyll's honest and damning description of Hyde and 'his' particular depth of darkness
10	'Instantly the spirit of hell awoke in me and raged.'	
10		Jekyll describes how the evil in Hyde makes it easy for him to act with no humanity or empathy for others

Calvinist a member of a major branch of the Protestant religion that follows the teaching of John Calvin; Stevenson was brought up in a Calvinist family

Mr Gabriel Utterson

A successful lawyer with distinguished clients and a solid reputation, Utterson is the character through whom the reader is introduced to the tragic tale of Dr Jekyll. He is portrayed as **conservative** and dependable, loyal to the friends he has maintained for many years and a respected professional. Concerned throughout for his friend Dr Jekyll, he ultimately discovers the truth about Hyde through his reading of Lanyon's letter and Jekyll's 'Full Statement'.

> **conservative** an attitude towards life that dislikes change and respects tradition

Activity 13

The key quotations below represent key aspects of the character that Stevenson needed for his narrator. Read again the first page or two of the novella and add characteristics and supporting quotations to the spider diagram below to build up a picture of Mr Utterson's essential nature.

> **Key quotations**
>
> '[...] the last reputable acquaintance and the last good influence in the lives of down-going men.' *(Chapter 1)*
>
> 'His friends were those of his own blood or those whom he had known the longest' *(Chapter 1)*

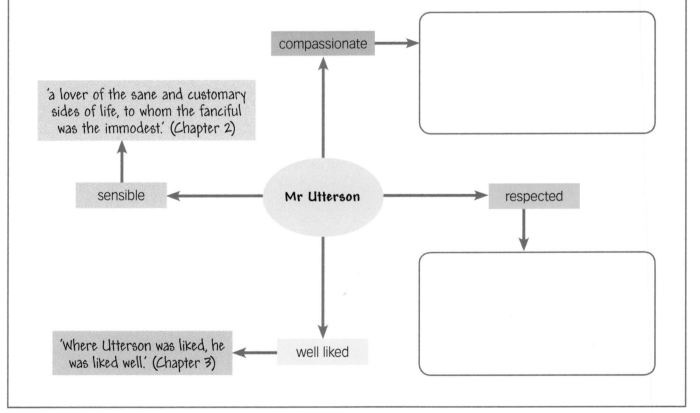

Activity 14

Utterson is absorbed with the fate of his friend Dr Jekyll once he has heard the story about Hyde from Mr Enfield. Look at the following list, which contains some of Utterson's thoughts and comments involving Dr Jekyll from the first five chapters. Place the quotations in the correct chronological order by including the chapter number in the column (where there is more than one quotation per chapter use 1a, 1b etc. to clarify).

Quotation	Chapter
'The lawyer listened gloomily; he did not like his friend's feverish manner.'	
'"What!" he thought. "Henry Jekyll forge for a murderer!"'	
"Ay, I must put my shoulder to the wheel – if Jekyll will but let me,"	
'[...] he was surprised at his friend's selfishness, and yet relieved by it.'	
'He thought of him kindly; but his thoughts were disquieted and fearful.'	

Activity 15

Write a short paragraph on a separate piece of paper to discuss the development of the thoughts of Utterson towards his friend in the first five chapters. How does his opinion of him change?

Activity 16

Utterson's character and his suspicions are used by Stevenson to manage the readers' suspense and to create a developing mystery that is only solved through the final words of Henry Jekyll. Select three decisions made by Utterson that are crucial to the development of the narrative and explain why.

Decision	How it affects the narrative
1.	
2.	
3.	

Dr Hastie Lanyon

Dr Lanyon is a friend of both Utterson and Dr Jekyll. He informs Utterson that he has long had doubts about Jekyll's research. His sudden death only a week after this meeting is a great shock, and it brings Utterson into the possession of the letter that explains that Lanyon had witnessed Hyde's transformation into Jekyll.

> **Key quotations**
>
> '[…] a hearty, healthy, dapper, red-faced gentleman' *(Chapter 2)*
>
> 'He had his death-warrant written legibly upon his face.' *(Chapter 6)*

Activity 17

Dr Lanyon's letter informs Utterson about everything that could not be explicitly explained in the earlier chapters. In the table below there are a number of comments from Dr Lanyon from the earlier chapters. Think about what he was hinting at but not able to explain fully and complete the table with what you think he really meant. The first is completed as an example. The last example may have a number of possible answers – read the final part of Chapter 9 before making your decision.

Lanyon's comment	What he really meant
"I see little of him now."	I do not really want to see him. Our friendship has cooled due to disagreements.
"[…] it is more than ten years since Henry Jekyll became too fanciful for me."	
"Well, life has been pleasant; I liked it; yes, sir, I used to like it."	
"I sometimes think if we knew all, we should be more glad to get away."	
"'Nothing can be done,' returned Lanyon; 'ask himself.'" *(referring to Jekyll)*	
"Some day, Utterson, after I am dead, you may perhaps come to learn the right and wrong of this. I cannot tell you."	

Activity 18

The relationship between Lanyon and Dr Jekyll clearly broke down due to a disagreement over scientific investigations and practice. Write a letter as Lanyon to Jekyll explaining your feelings about the nature of his research. This could be the letter that fractured their friendship and left Jekyll feeling that Lanyon thought he was losing his mind. Use a separate piece of paper. You may wish to consider including the following points:

- Lanyon's feelings that Jekyll should restrict himself to traditional science
- explaining that Jekyll's ideas are starting to make him think he can act like God
- reminding him that he is a lesser scientist by reputation and that he should listen to Lanyon and take his advice.

Mr Richard Enfield

Mr Richard Enfield regularly accompanies Utterson on Sunday walks and he is the first to mention Hyde in the novella. He shares the unsettling experience of witnessing Jekyll's **"expression of such abject terror and despair"** *(Chapter 7)* at a window above the alley.

> **Key quotations**
>
> **"I had taken a loathing to my gentleman at first sight."** *(Chapter 1)*
>
> **'"Well," said Enfield, "that story's at an end at least. We shall never see more of Mr Hyde."'** *(Chapter 7)*

Activity 19

Look at the words in the following table and explain why you feel each is a relevant description of Enfield's character and/or behaviour by referring to the text. One has been completed as an example.

Adjective	Relevance to Enfield in the novella
relative	The text refers to Enfield as Utterson's 'distant kinsman' – earlier stating that his friends were 'those of his own blood'
secretive	
loyal	
outraged	
assertive	
appalled	
resourceful	
mysterious	

Poole

Poole is Jekyll's loyal butler. He tells Utterson he has to take orders from Hyde in his master's absence but asks for his help when Jekyll behaves strangely and will not leave his room. He witnesses the discovery of the body of Hyde.

> **Key quotations**
>
> "We have all orders to obey him." *(Chapter 2 – referring to Hyde)*
>
> "[...] put your heart in your ears Mr Utterson, and tell me, is that the doctor's foot?" *(Chapter 8)*

Activity 20

There is a clear difference between the way Poole is portrayed in the earlier chapters and the time when he independently seeks the help of Utterson at the beginning of Chapter 8.

On a separate piece of paper write a paragraph exploring the changing role of Poole in the novella and the ways in which Stevenson develops and concentrates his importance in Chapter 8. You may wish to revisit the following as you consider the role of Poole:

- first appearance and comments in Chapter 2
- brief role in Chapter 5
- his initial request in Chapter 8
- his emotional state
- the way he talks to the other servants
- knowledge of the drugs and chemicals ordered by Jekyll
- not recognizing Jekyll
- breaking into the cabinet and finding Hyde's body
- witnessing the changed will benefiting Utterson
- passing on the letters and awaiting Utterson's return before calling the police.

Other characters

The other characters play much smaller roles in the narrative: Mr Guest, head clerk at Mr Utterson's legal practice; Inspector Newcomen, the police officer who reports the death of Sir Danvers Carew; Bradshaw, the footman; and Dr Jekyll's and Hyde's housekeeper in Soho.

Activity 21

Use the table below to include details of the minor characters. One has been completed for you as an example, though you can add more detail.

Character	Role	Quotation	Quality/trait
Mr Guest	Head clerk	'[...] a great student and critic of handwriting'	Professional skill in graphology
Inspector Newcomen			
Bradshaw			
Hyde's housekeeper			

 Progress check

Use the chart below to review the skills you have developed in this chapter. For each column, start at the bottom box and work your way up towards the highest level in the top box. Tick the box to show you have achieved that level.

I can sustain a critical response to *Jekyll and Hyde* and interpret the themes convincingly ☐	I can analyse the effects of Stevenson's use of language, structure and form in *Jekyll and Hyde*, using subject terms judiciously ☐	I can use well-integrated textual references from *Jekyll and Hyde* to support my interpretation ☐	I use a wide range of vocabulary and can spell and punctuate consistently accurately ☐
I can develop a coherent response to *Jekyll and Hyde* and explain the language clearly ☐	I can explain how Stevenson uses language, structure and form to create effects in *Jekyll and Hyde*, using relevant subject terms ☐	I can use quotations and other textual references from *Jekyll and Hyde* to support my explanation ☐	I use a range of vocabulary and can spell and punctuate, mostly accurately ☐
I can make some comments on the language in *Jekyll and Hyde* ☐	I can identify some of Stevenson's methods in *Jekyll and Hyde* and use some subject terms ☐	I can make references to some details from *Jekyll and Hyde* ☐	I use a simple range of vocabulary and spell and punctuate with some accuracy ☐
Personal response	**Language, structure, form**	**Textual references**	**Technical accuracy**

53

Writing about language

Many students are led to believe that GCSE English Literature essays need to be filled with detailed analysis of language and identification of literary terms in order to score marks in the higher bands. This often leads to very able students writing essays that *do not answer the question* but are instead filled with language analysis. Remember, you should only identify the use of a literary device such as a **simile** or **metaphor** if it supports the development of your answer.

metaphor a figure of speech applied to something to suggest a resemblance without using the words 'like' or 'as'

simile a figure of speech applied to something to suggest a resemblance, introduced by the words 'like' or 'as'

Use of metaphor

The novella contains some powerful images. The power of the imagery to trigger the reader's imagination to move beyond the literal is a key part of Stevenson's skill as a novelist. One way metaphor is used vividly is to portray Hyde and the effect of his character on others.

Activity 1

Look at the table below and comment on how you think the use of metaphor strengthens the description. The first one has been done for you.

Chapter	Metaphor	Effect
1	'[...] under a weight of consideration.'	By focusing the seriousness of the information into the image of a weight, the writer successfully portrays the heavy heart and sinking feeling that Utterson is experiencing due to his knowledge that Hyde is the man mentioned in Jekyll's will.
1	'[...] the two men put the greatest store by these excursions, counted them the chief jewel of each week'	
4	'[...] a great flame of anger'	
9	"[...] the shipwreck of my reason."	
7	'[...] froze the very blood of the two gentlemen below.'	
10	'[...] shook the very fortress of identity'	
10	'[...] shook the doors of the prisonhouse of my disposition'	
10	'[...] spring headlong into the sea of liberty.'	

Use of simile

Stevenson's use of simile is relatively straightforward and creates some very direct and vivid images. Stevenson uses simile to describe and enhance both characters and inanimate (non-living) subjects in the novella. When writing about the use of language in an exam answer, remember to distinguish between the use of simile and metaphor and make sensible comments about the effect of their use rather than just identifying that they exist.

Activity 2

a) Look at the following examples of similes used in the novella. Note down next to each what it refers to:

'[...] his affections, like ivy, were the growth of time.' *(Chapter 1)* — Utterson

'[shop fronts] like rows of smiling saleswomen.' *(Chapter 1)* —

'[the street] like a fire in a forest' *(Chapter 1)* —

"[women] as wild as harpies." *(Chapter 1)* —

"[the doctor] about as emotional as a bagpipe." *(Chapter 1)* —

"[...] it was like some damned Juggernaut." *(Chapter 1)* — Hyde

'[...] ape-like fury' *(Chapter 4)* — Hyde

'[...] like a district of some city in a nightmare.' *(Chapter 4)* —

'[...] where the lamps glimmered like carbuncles' *(Chapter 5)* —

'[...] like some disconsolate prisoner' *(Chapter 7)* — Jekyll

'[...] the whole of the servants, men and women, stood huddled together like a flock of sheep.' *(Chapter 8)* —

"[...] the hair stood upon my head like quills." *(Chapter 8)* —

'A dismal screech, as of mere animal terror' *(Chapter 8)* —

'Edward Hyde would pass away like the stain of breath upon a mirror' *(Chapter 10)* —

b) Choose five similes that you feel to be the most effective and use the table below to record your thoughts about how each one improves the description.

Chapter	Simile	Effect

Personification

The use of personification in the novella introduces a sense of humanity to inanimate or abstract (non-physical) subjects. It can be argued that the use of **personification** adds a poetic energy to descriptions as it creates a sense of real and living character.

personification when human qualities are given to something non-human, such as an object or idea

You should always explain the effect of a literary device such as personification, e.g. that the power of the image is intensified for the reader.

Activity 3

There are some examples of personification used in the novella by Stevenson below.
Draw lines to match each quotation with the correct explanation/analysis.

Quotation

'[...] it began to be clothed upon with detestable attributes' *(Chapter 2)*

'Instantly the spirit of hell awoke in me and raged.' *(Chapter 10)*

'[...] a haggard shaft of daylight would glance in between the swirling wreaths.' *(Chapter 4)*

'[...] a certain sinister block of building thrust forward its gable on the street.' *(Chapter 1)*

'[...] a week ago, the prospect had smiled with every promise' *(Chapter 6)*

'[...] the red baize door leaped against the lock and hinges.' *(Chapter 8)*

'[...] the packet slept in the inmost corner of his private safe.' *(Chapter 6)*

'[...] and the thin trees in the garden were lashing themselves along the railing.' *(Chapter 8)*

'[...] by the light of a melancholy candle' *(Chapter 6)*

'The fog still slept on the wing above the drowned city' *(Chapter 5)*

Explanation/analysis

The door is described as if acting of its own accord though the force is creating the movement.

The effect of the description is an emphasis on the disappointment that things were reverting to the way they were before his apparent recovery.

The sense that the document is at rest, waiting to be read, leaves the reader in anticipation, wondering what secrets it holds.

Although the source of light in the room, the description goes beyond this and gives it the emotion of sadness to match his mood.

The weather is reflecting the mood of Utterson. He is feeling as if he is being battered by the events surrounding Jekyll and anxious at what he will find.

Knowing the description of Hyde after hearing Enfield's story has started his imagination working to picture Hyde for himself.

The building is portrayed as intrusive and almost forcing itself upon the passers-by. The writer is drawing the reader's attention to the back door of Jekyll's house for it will play an important role.

The weather is portrayed at rest but it is smothering the city like a shroud.

The light is depicted as travel-weary and exhausted, trying to find a way through the fog. The power of evil is given life in this description and emphasizes his lack of control.

The power of evil is given life in this description and emphasises his lack of control.

Activity 4

At the end of Chapter 9, Dr Lanyon recounts his feelings of horror after having witnessed the physical transformation of Hyde into Jekyll. This extract is the final part of his account.

> What he told me in the next hour, I cannot bring my mind to set on paper. I saw what I saw, I heard what I heard, and my soul sickened at it; and yet now when that sight has faded from my eyes, I ask myself if I believe it, and I cannot answer. My life is shaken to its roots; sleep has left me; the deadliest terror sits by me at all hours of the day and night; I feel that my days are numbered, and that I must die; and yet I shall die incredulous. As for the moral turpitude that man unveiled to me, even with tears of penitence, I cannot, even in memory, dwell on it without a start of horror. I will say but one thing, Utterson, and that (if you can bring your mind to credit it) will be more than enough. The creature who crept into my house that night was, on Jekyll's own confession, known by the name of Hyde and hunted for in every corner of the land as the murderer of Carew.
> *(Chapter 9)*

a) Highlight all the instances of personification you can find in the extract.

b) How does the writer's use of personification in this paragraph make the character's feelings more intense for the reader?

Dialogue

Dialogue is used for various reasons in the novella: it develops characters through their use of language, it introduces a surprising or shocking turn of events in the narrative and it increases the level of intrigue and enquiry in the mind of the reader. What characters do not say is also important as it adds to the sense of mystery in the novella.

dialogue conversation in a book, play or film

Activity 5

The table below contains some extracts from dialogue in the novella. Consider the significance of each extract – the first one has been completed for you. You may want to consider the following points:

- What does it tell us about the character speaking? What language are they using, what views are they expressing?

- Does it tell us anything about the other characters?

- How does it develop the narrative?

- Is there anything the character is not saying? What effect does this have?

Dialogue extract	Chapter	Significance
"Did you ever remark that door?" he asked; and when his companion had replied in the affirmative, "It is connected in my mind," added he, "with a very odd story."	1	This certainly introduces Enfield's character as someone more talkative than we expected. It also pulls both Utterson and the reader along, intrigued by the 'odd story' and plants a sense of mystery right at the start of the novella.
"The fact is, if I do not ask you the name of the other party, it is because I know it already."	1	
"But it is more than ten years since Henry Jekyll became too fanciful for me. He began to go wrong, wrong in mind"	2	
"He never told you," cried Mr Hyde, with a flush of anger. "I did not think you would have lied."	2	
"Yes sir, he do indeed," said Poole. "We have all orders to obey him."	2	
"O, I know he's a good fellow – you needn't frown – an excellent fellow, and I always mean to see more of him; but a hide-bound pedant for all that"	3	
"I don't ask that," pleaded Jekyll, laying his hand upon the other's arm; "I only ask you to help him for my sake, when I am no longer here."	3	
"Yes," said he, "I recognise him. I am sorry to say that this is Sir Danvers Carew."	4	
'A flash of odious joy appeared upon the woman's face. "Ah!" said she, "he is in trouble! What has he done?"'	4	
"Well, sir," returned the clerk, "there's a rather singular resemblance; the two hands are in many points identical: only differently sloped."	5	

Activity 6

Write a paragraph discussing the importance of dialogue in the novella. You now have plenty of examples to reference but choose carefully – don't rewrite complete quotations instead use selected words and phrases. Discuss the ways in which the dialogue affects how the reader may react to the characters involved.

Use some of the following words to help you analyse the importance of dialogue:

surprising   engaging   conversation   friendship

shock   emotional   thoughtful   reflective   stern

respectful   assertive   desperate   passionate

curious   hint   suggestion   characterize(s/ed)

Upgrade

Don't fall into the trap of writing essays that focus only on your knowledge of literary devices and their effects – these may all be valid points but will tend to miss the aim of the question. Don't leave examiners waiting for you to refer to the subject of the question.

The language of science

For a narrative that deals with the physical transformation of a human being, there is a limited amount of scientific discussion in the text. However, in Chapter 9 in particular, the reader is exposed to some scientific terminology when we learn about Jekyll (as Hyde) transforming in front of Dr Lanyon.

> **Key quotation**
>
> '[...] I will not enter deeply into this scientific branch of my confession.'
> *(Chapter 10)*

Activity 7

A modern reader will be far more familiar with the language of science and scientific terms than Victorian readers would have been. However, there is a very focused number of terms used in Chapter 9. Research their meaning so that you have a clear idea of what they describe and why they are mentioned in the text.

Scientific word/phrase	Meaning – in context
'crystalline salt'	
'phial'	
'pungent'	
'phosphorus'	
'volatile ether'	
'a graduated glass'	
'a few minims'	
'tincture'	
'effervesce audibly'	
'small fumes of vapour'	
'ebullition'	
'compound'	

The language describing Hyde

The terms used to describe Edward Hyde vary across the novella with most referring to stature and appearance. The final chapter allows the character of Jekyll to reflect on his work and regrets. Stevenson uses the 'Statement' to create an **internal monologue** for Jekyll where he views Hyde and explores his feelings from a number of perspectives.

> **internal monologue** a literary device where a character's thoughts are presented as speech

Activity 8

The following quotations used to describe Hyde are a few examples of the way in which he is objectified and portrayed as something to be feared. Complete the table by identifying the linguistic technique used and the effect this has. You may want to look for the following: metaphor, simile, personification, oxymoron, alliteration, repetition.

Quotation	Chapter	Linguistic technique	Effect
"[...] your sight shall be blasted by a prodigy"	9	Metaphor	Warning Lanyon that his 'sight will be blasted' emphasizes the profound effect that witnessing the transformation will have by suggesting that he will be blind to everything after this.
'[...] that ugly idol'	10		
'This familiar that I called out'	10		
'[...] the animal within me licking the chops of memory'	10		
'That child of Hell had nothing human; nothing lived in him but fear and hatred.'	10		
'[...] the brute that slept within me'	10		
'[...] something not only hellish but inorganic'	10		
'[...] that the slime of the pit seemed to utter cries and voices; that the amorphous dust gesticulated and sinned'	10		
'[...] relentless like a man of stone.'	10		
'[...] a sort of murderous mixture of timidity and boldness'	2		
'A dismal screech, as of mere animal terror, rang from the cabinet.'	8		

Activity 9

Research other terms used to describe Hyde in the novella. You should be able to find up to 20 more. Write these terms in your notebook.

Activity 10

In this activity you need to think about the way that Stevenson has used language to portray Jekyll's feelings about Hyde in the final two chapters. Write a paragraph to explain your thoughts. Remember to use short integrated quotations to support the points you make.

Upgrade

Your knowledge of language techniques is like a toolkit – you have to select wisely so that you get the job done well. The final result should be a well-structured essay that is focused on the question, explains the effect of techniques appropriately and is completed in the limited time you have in an exam!

Creating tension and suspense

Stevenson effectively creates a tense atmosphere and keeps the readers in suspense, eager for the mystery to be revealed. He does this in various ways, through structure and character, but also through his language choices.

Activity 11

Tension and suspense build up throughout the novella as readers are presented with ever more questions and no answers. Hyde's transformation into Jekyll is the revelation the reader has been waiting for. With this in mind, look at the passage below taken from Chapter 9, 'Dr Lanyon's Narrative'.

> He put the glass to his lips and drank at one gulp. A cry followed; he reeled, staggered, clutched at the table and held on, staring with injected eyes, gasping with open mouth; and as I looked there came, I thought, a change – he seemed to swell – his face became suddenly black and the features seemed to melt and alter – and the next moment, I had sprung to my feet and leaped back against the wall, my arm raised to shield me from that prodigy, my mind submerged in terror.
>
> 'O God!' I screamed, and 'O God!' again and again; for there before my eyes – pale and shaken, and half fainting, and groping before him with his hands, like a man restored from death – there stood Henry Jekyll!
>
> *(Chapter 9)*

Explain how Stevenson uses each of the following techniques in this extract to build tension. Use short quotations to support your ideas.

Sentence length:

Punctuation:

Repetition:

Activity 12

Tension and suspense are heightened on many occasions in the novella. Look at the following quotations and suggest how you feel that the language adds to the tension and suspense.

Quotation	Effect
"I thought it was madness... and now I begin to fear it is disgrace." *(Chapter 2)*	
"if ever I read Satan's signature upon a face, it is on that of your new friend." *(Chapter 2)*	
'At the horror of these sights and sounds, the maid fainted.' *(Chapter 4)*	
'And his blood ran cold in his veins.' *(Chapter 5)*	
'"Weeping? how that?" said the lawyer, conscious of a sudden chill of horror.' *(Chapter 8)*	
"it only remains for us to find the body of your master." *(Chapter 8)*	

Unfamiliar vocabulary

In 1885, Stevenson wrote in some detail about the craft and art of writing, the same year in which he finished composing *The Strange Case of Dr Jekyll and Mr Hyde*. The most important point he makes is focused on writers being able to piece together the right words in the right place, what he calls the 'springs and mechanisms', so that the reader appreciates the beauty of the finished work. The problem for most modern readers is that many of the words he used make understanding the text more difficult because of the unfamiliar vocabulary. Therefore, some time is needed to research unfamiliar words so that the original meaning in context can be understood and the skill and artistry of the writer fully appreciated.

Activity 13

Create your own dictionary to help you understand and recall some of the words and phrases that you find difficult in the novella. A few from the first two chapters have been placed in the table below to get you started. Then develop your notes on words and phrases as you read the text. In the end they will hopefully become more familiar and you will be able to discuss the effect of the vocabulary choice with confidence.

Word/phrase	Chapter	Meaning – in context
'embarrassed in discourse'	1	Conversation – Mr Utterson found it difficult to chat to people in general
'sordid negligence'	1	The building was dirty and had been badly neglected for some time
'the whole business looked apocryphal'	1	This means that Enfield doubted that the cheque handed to him by Hyde was authentic – and was a forgery
'The will was holograph'	2	This means that Dr Jekyll's will had been handwritten by him and not the lawyer (who dislikes its contents)
'through wider labyrinths'	2	The streets of London are being compared to the complicated maze from Greek mythology
'the picture of disquietude'	2	
'mental perplexity'	2	
'scientific heresies'	3	
'insensate cruelty'	4	
'odious joy'	4	
'out of the ken of the police'	6	
'emphatically superscribed'	6	

Progress check

Use the chart below to review the skills you have developed in this chapter. For each column, start at the bottom box and work your way up towards the highest level in the top box. Tick the box to show you have achieved that level.

I can analyse the effects of Stevenson's use of language, structure and form in *Jekyll and Hyde*, using subject terms judiciously ☐	I can use well-integrated textual references from *Jekyll and Hyde* to support my interpretation ☐	I use a wide range of vocabulary and can spell and punctuate consistently accurately ☐
I can explain how Stevenson uses language, structure and form to create effects in *Jekyll and Hyde*, using relevant subject terms ☐	I can use quotations and other textual references from *Jekyll and Hyde* to support my explanation ☐	I use a range of vocabulary and can spell and punctuate, mostly accurately ☐
I can identify some of Stevenson's methods in *Jekyll and Hyde* and use some subject terms ☐	I can make references to some details from *Jekyll and Hyde* ☐	I use a simple range of vocabulary and spell and punctuate with some accuracy ☐
Language, structure, form	**Textual references**	**Technical accuracy**

Social class in Victorian England

Victorian society was governed by a strict social **hierarchy**. The upper middle classes would consider themselves to be entitled to respect from the lower, middle and working classes. Education was also important in dividing the classes, and codes of conduct were put in place to differentiate those who had been taught at a particular level and those who had not. The concept of being seen as an **honourable** 'gentleman' was critically important in terms of class; it signalled not only social status but also the assumption of a high level of morality and fairness towards others.

> **hierarchy** a system of ranking according to birth, status and authority, etc.
>
> **honourable** having the respect of others due to previous reputation and behaviour

Activity 1

Write a paragraph explaining your thoughts about why Stevenson selected his main protagonists from a relatively high level of Victorian society.

You may wish to include:

- their professions
- the respect they have earned from their peers
- the readership at the time
- the standards of behaviour/morality they expect from others.

Remember to use short integrated quotations to support the points you make.

Activity 2

All of the main protagonists in the novella are portrayed as gentlemen. The narrative is initially set in a world of politeness, restraint and the avoidance of scandal until it is shaken by the disruption of Hyde. Look at the following table, which includes some references to class from the novella. Note who or what you think is being described and how the quotation can be related to class. They are not placed in chronological order.

Quotation	Who/what is being described	Reference to class
'[…] with its muddy ways, and slatternly passengers' *(Chapter 4)*		
"[…] the person that drew the cheque is the very pink of the proprieties" *(Chapter 1)*		
'[…] with every guarantee of an honourable and distinguished future.' *(Chapter 10)*		
"[…] we could and would make such a scandal out of this" *(Chapter 1)*		
'[…] it seemed to breathe such an innocent and old-world kindness of disposition, yet with something high too' *(Chapter 4)*		
"You might suppose, after this preface, that I am going to ask you for something dishonourable" *(Chapter 9)*		
'[…] now for the most part decayed from their high estate and let in flats and chambers to all sorts and conditions of men' *(Chapter 2)*		
"[…] was that my master's voice?" *(Chapter 8)*		
'[…] many ragged children huddled in the doorways' *(Chapter 4)*		

Duality in human nature

The basic principle of most religious beliefs is the presence of both positive and negative forces in the world. These forces have been personified in different forms of 'good' and 'evil' throughout time. Furthermore, all individuals have the capacity to act for both forces; however, the 'evil' desires are kept in check by the morally 'good' character of the person who was taught the difference between what society sees as 'right' and 'wrong' from a young age.

In the novella it could be argued that Stevenson is suggesting that evil must be contained, otherwise it will take control of a person's **psyche** and become invincible. The novella, written towards the end of the 19th century, was read by a largely Christian readership. Robert Louis Stevenson was himself brought up as a strict Calvinist with a deep terror of evil and sin; it was impossible for him to deny that evil was not deep-rooted in the world. From this perspective, Edward Hyde represents the evil in every person.

> **psyche** the human mind (and spirit – from a religious perspective)

Key quotations

'[…] I stood already committed to a profound duplicity of life.'
(Chapter 10 – Jekyll referring to his two distinct characters – before the emergence of Hyde)

'Though so profound a double-dealer, I was in no sense a hypocrite;'
(Chapter 10 – as above)

At the beginning of the final chapter, Dr Jekyll attempts to rationalize his actions in separating the two diverse sides of human nature. In some sense he is perhaps looking for forgiveness as much as understanding. The reader is aware of the Dr Lanyon's reaction to the scientific proof of Jekyll's discoveries, and that with his work, Jekyll had been judged by Lanyon to have gone too far. Lanyon believes he has strayed into the territory that was reserved for God (i.e. the creator – from a Christian perspective).

Activity 3

Read again the following extract from the beginning of Chapter 10. The highlighted passages are referenced in questions on page 72, which are designed to develop your understanding and to put Jekyll's ideas under some closer scrutiny.
Use a dictionary to help you with some of the more unfamiliar terms.

With every day, and from both sides of my intelligence, the moral and the intellectual, I thus drew steadily nearer to that truth, by whose partial discovery I have been doomed to such a dreadful shipwreck: that man is not truly one, but truly two. I say two, because the state of my own knowledge does not pass beyond that point. Others will follow, others will outstrip me on the same lines; and I hazard the guess that man will be ultimately known for a mere polity of multifarious, incongruous and independent denizens. I for my part, from the nature of my life, advanced infallibly in one direction and in one direction only. It was on the moral side, and in my own person, that I learned to recognise the thorough and primitive duality of man; I saw that, of the two natures that contended in the field of my consciousness, even if I could rightly be said to be either, it was only because I was radically both; and from an early date, even before the course of my scientific discoveries had begun to suggest the most naked possibility of such a miracle, I had learned to dwell with pleasure, as a beloved daydream, on the thought of the separation of these elements. If each, I told myself, could but be housed in separate identities, life would be relieved of all that was unbearable; the unjust might go his way, delivered from the aspirations and remorse of his more upright twin; and the just could walk steadfastly and securely on his upward path, doing the good things in which he found his pleasure, and no longer exposed to disgrace and penitence by the hands of this extraneous evil. It was the curse of mankind that these incongruous faggots were thus bound together – that in the agonised womb of consciousness, these polar twins should be continuously struggling. How, then were they dissociated?

I was so far in my reflections when, as I have said, a side light began to shine upon the subject from the laboratory table. I began to perceive more deeply than it has ever yet been stated, the trembling immateriality, the mist-like transience, of this seemingly so solid body in which we walk attired. Certain agents I found to have the power to shake and to pluck back that fleshly vestment, even as a wind might toss the curtains of a pavilion. For two good reasons, I will not enter deeply into this scientific branch of my confession. First, because I have been made to learn that the doom and burthen of our life is bound for ever on man's shoulders, and when the attempt is made to cast it off, it but returns upon us with more unfamiliar and more awful pressure. Second, because, as my narrative will make alas! too evident, my discoveries were incomplete.

(Chapter 10)

a) Why do you think Jekyll stresses that the 'truth', as he sees it, has been looked at from both a 'moral and intellectual' perspective?

----

b) How does Jekyll think that this research will be continued and what does this tell us about his views on the duality of man?

----

c) What justification for his investigations is suggested by 'because I was radically both'?

----

d) What does he believe to be so particularly 'unbearable' about life that it needs to be 'relieved'? How is this linked to 'the curse of mankind'?

----

e) How do the words 'the trembling immateriality, the mist-like transience' begin to show that Jekyll had started to view the human body ('his fleshly vestment') from a different perspective?

----

f) Explain the first reason he gives for not wanting to divulge specific details about how he managed successfully to separate himself into 'two' distinct parts.

The influence of religion

The role of religion as a defence against the forces of evil was very important in Victorian society. The majority of the population would attend church on Sundays, believe in God and Christian teachings, as well as own bibles and other religious works for education and worship. The universal nature of religion helped to empower the Church and maintain its influence in society through **scriptures** used in the education of children and prayers said before court hearings and political meetings at all levels. As a result of this widespread influence of religion, everyday speech was full of references to God, something still true today (though often not underpinned by a belief or faith). Its use then would have had a more profound impact.

> **scripture** religious text used in church, home and school

Activity 4

Below are some examples of references to God and religion throughout the novella in the chronological order of their appearance. Note what you feel to be the reason for the reference at that point in the text. The first one is completed for you as an example.

a) '[...] a volume of some dry divinity on his reading desk' *(Chapter 2)*

This refers to the fact that Utterson (as a Christian) would usually read a religious text on a Sunday but the meeting with Hyde has upset him so much that he has decided to reread Jekyll's will.

b) "God bless me, the man seems hardly human" *(Chapter 2)*

----

c) '[...] but in the law of God, there is no statute of limitations' *(Chapter 2)*

----

d) '"I swear to God," cried the doctor, "I swear to God I will never set eyes on him again."' *(Chapter 5)*

----

e) '[...] and whilst he had always been known for charities, he was now
no less distinguished for religion.' *(Chapter 6)*

----

f) '"[...] and God grant there be nothing wrong."
"Amen, Poole," said the lawyer.' *(Chapter 8)*

----

g) "[...] and I give you my bible-word it was Mr Hyde!" *(Chapter 8)*

----

h) '[...] a copy of a pious work... annotated, in his own hand, with startling
blasphemies.' *(Chapter 8)*

----

i) '"O God!" I screamed, and "O God!" again and again' *(Chapter 9)*

----

j) '[...] I sought with tears and prayers to smother down the crowd of
hideous images and sounds' *(Chapter 10)*

----

k) '[...] Henry Jekyll, with streaming tears of gratitude and remorse, had fallen upon his knees and lifted his clasped hands to God.' *(Chapter 10)*

Upgrade

In your assessment, you may be asked to write specifically about a theme like religion, class or friendship, or you may have to discuss the themes presented in a given extract or scene. When writing about themes, remember to offer clear examples from throughout the text to support your ideas and strengthen your argument.

Activity 5

On a separate piece of paper, write a paragraph to explain how religion underpins some of the characters' thoughts in the novella. Use some of the references you have explored in Activity 4 to help you.

You may wish to mention:

- references to religious writing
- emotions that lead characters to exclaim the name of 'God'
- references to prayer
- acknowledging God as a protector.

Remember to use short integrated quotations to support the points you make.

Friendship and loyalty

The friendship between the main male characters is a significant aspect of the narrative. On the first page we learn that Utterson tends to maintain long-term relationships. The loyalty shown by Utterson towards Jekyll is contrasted by Dr Lanyon's rejection of Jekyll after disagreeing with the nature of his research. However, even among professed friends, their level of knowledge about each other is surprisingly limited. In a sense this reflects the Victorian respect for privacy.

> **Key quotations**
>
> '[...] men who thoroughly enjoyed each other's company.'
> *(Chapter 2)*
>
> "[...] you and I must be the two oldest friends that Henry Jekyll has?"
> *(Chapter 2 – Utterson speaking to Dr Lanyon)*
>
> "We are three very old friends, Lanyon; we shall not live to make others."
> *(Chapter 6)*

Activity 6

Mr Utterson is the central figure and link in terms of the web of friendship in the novella.

a) Use the spider diagram below to show the links between Utterson's friends. You should draw arrows between the names to indicate the links. You could use a broken line to indicate a damaged friendship.

b) Next add information about the friendships between each character. Some points for Utterson and Enfield have already been added.

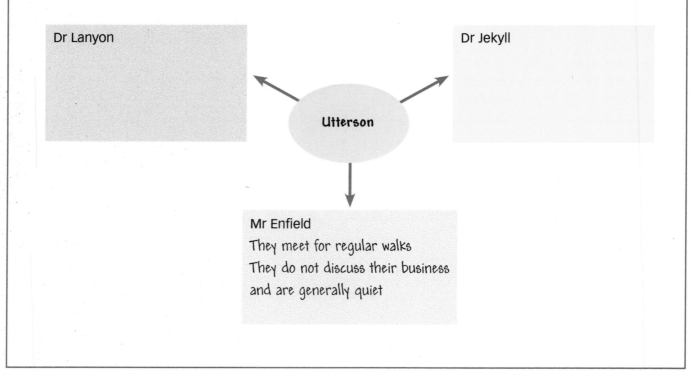

Dr Lanyon

Dr Jekyll

Utterson

Mr Enfield
They meet for regular walks
They do not discuss their business and are generally quiet

Activity 7

Dr Jekyll informs Utterson towards the end of Chapter 3 that **"I would trust you before any man alive"**. If this was the case, why do you think Jekyll chose Dr Lanyon (rather than Utterson) to retrieve the drawer of chemicals from the cabinet and take them to Cavendish Square? Write a paragraph on a separate piece of paper to answer this, using quotations to support your points.

You may wish to remind yourself about the beginning of Chapters 2, 3 and 9 where the friendships are portrayed through thoughts, dialogue and letter.

The power of documents

The power of the written word through both legal and private documents influences and drives the narrative throughout the novella (e.g. Guest's identification of Jekyll's distinctive handwriting at the end of Chapter 5). By using documents written in the 'voice' of different characters, Stevenson adopts the useful device of offering the reader extended accounts from alternative narrators. The character who receives all the documents is Utterson, both as professional lawyer and friend of Lanyon and Jekyll. We read these documents at the same time as Utterson and so our understanding of what has happened is shared.

Activity 8

The list below details the main documents referenced in the novella. Consider the importance of each of these documents for the reader. What do we learn from them and what do they show us? Note down your thoughts after each document. The first one has been done for you.

a) 'Dr Jekyll's Will' – introduced and read in Chapter 2

> The fact that this is a legal document where Jekyll is naming Hyde as the man to inherit his wealth, shows how close these two characters must be. It also makes Utterson suspect the nature of their relationship and whether blackmail may be involved.

b) The note (apparently from Hyde suggesting his disappearance for good) shown to Utterson by Jekyll – later identified by Mr Guest as having actually been written by Jekyll – in Chapter 5

----

c) Jekyll's note to Messrs Maw, shown to Utterson by Poole at the beginning of Chapter 8

----

d) The new will naming Utterson as beneficiary discovered in Jekyll's cabinet in Chapter 8

----

e) The letter marked 'PRIVATE' from Dr Lanyon to Utterson, which is the account referenced by Jekyll (introduced in Chapter 6 though not read until Chapter 9)

----

f) The letter from Jekyll requesting Lanyon's help, which is placed ahead of Lanyon's detailed account at the beginning of Chapter 9

---

g) Jekyll's detailed account of his scientific experiments and struggles with losing control of Hyde given in 'Henry Jekyll's Full Statement of the Case' in Chapter 10

Activity 9

Look at another one of the documents in the novella: the extract from the notebook recording Jekyll's experiments and Lanyon's thoughts, described in Chapter 9. The extract begins with 'The book was an ordinary version book' and ends with 'I loaded an old revolver'.

Explain what clues are being given to the reader in this document.

Secrets and lies

The whole narrative is filled with guarded secrets and lies. Without them, the narrative would lose its energy and sense of mystery. As the reader, we discover particular information at certain times. However, beyond this, there are secrets kept and deliberate lies told within the novella, which necessarily remain unanswered until the revelations contained in the final two chapters. At times, the frustrated reader wishes that more questions were asked but the fact that we still seek answers drives the narrative forward.

> **Key quotation**
>
> **'There was no man from whom he kept fewer secrets than Mr Guest; and he was not always sure that he kept as many as he meant.'**
> *(Chapter 5)*

Activity 10

In the first two chapters, secrets and lies play a significant part in setting the scene of the novella, driving the narrative and engaging the interest of the reader. The columns below contain some selected references to secrets and lies from Chapters 1 and 2. However, both the references and the explanations are listed out of order.

a) Draw lines between the matching references and explanations.

b) Find further examples from Chapters 3 to 10 of where secrets and lies play significant roles in the development of the novella and explain their importance. Continue onto separate paper if you need to.

References	Explanations
'[…] it was his ignorance of Mr Hyde that had swelled his indignation'	Not reporting Hyde to the police at this point allowed Jekyll (as Hyde) to continue to behave recklessly and ultimately to commit the murder of Sir Danvers Carew.
'I did not think you would have lied.'	Utterson does not press Lanyon for more details after this mysterious statement because he does not see that a disagreement over a 'point of science' is important. It is possible that Lanyon may have told him more.
'[…] as should make his name stink from one end of London to the other.'	Utterson assumes that the secrets of Hyde must be far worse than his friend – and at this point, the reader has no reason to doubt his conclusion.
'Mr Utterson sighed deeply but said never a word'	This assumes that everyone will have secrets that could be used against them if made public – perhaps leading to a scandal.
'[…] secrets compared to which poor Jekyll's worst would be like sunshine.'	Hyde struggles to understand how Utterson knows that he is a 'friend' of Jekyll. It is interesting to note just how insulted Utterson feels at Hyde's accusation!
'Black mail, I suppose; an honest man paying through the nose for some of the capers of his youth.'	Utterson is angry that he had no knowledge of Mr Hyde other than his name in Jekyll's will.
'He began to go wrong, wrong in mind'	Utterson deliberately neglects to tell Enfield that Hyde is the main beneficiary of Jekyll's will, even though Enfield has recounted Hyde's trampling of the young girl and his reaction.

Activity 11

Write a paragraph on a separate piece of paper explaining the importance of Stevenson's use of secrets and lies in the development of the narrative of the novella.

The spirit of place

The environments described in the novella have an important role to play in the way that mood is established. From the alleyway in the first chapter to the descriptions of the different houses and the streets of London at night, the reader is led through a series of distinct and often **evocative** settings. The sophistication of the wealthy houses is countered by the poverty of the streets of Soho. Stevenson brings Victorian London to life and the spirit (or character) of each place creates a particular world in the mind of the reader.

> **evocative** creating strong images and/or feelings

Activity 12

The following table contains a selection of descriptions of place from the first five chapters. The quotations are listed in chronological order but you will need to locate them carefully to absorb the full context.

Explain what you learn about the place described, for example:

- physical details
- mood and atmosphere
- colours and temperature
- anything else that you feel has relevance.

One example is completed to give an idea of the kind of response you may note.

Quotation	Chapter	Significance
'[...] a by-street in a busy quarter of London.'	1	This is where we find the door from the rear of Jekyll's house. It is a lower social area, hidden from the more expensive houses on the square and is appropriate as Hyde's exit and entry.
'The door, which was equipped with neither bell nor knocker, was blistered and distained.'	1	
'Cavendish Square, that citadel of medicine'	2	
'[a] comfortable hall... furnished with costly cabinets of oak.'	2	
'[...] like a district of some city in a nightmare.'	4	
'[...] the carpets were of many plies and agreeable in colour.'	4	
'[...] looking out upon the court by three dusty windows barred with iron.'	5	

'[…] a dingy street, a gin palace, a low French eating house, a shop for the retail of penny numbers and twopenny salads'
(Chapter 4 – Soho)

'[…] he eyed the dingy windowless structure with curiosity, and gazed round with a distasteful sense of strangeness as he crossed the theatre'
(Chapter 5 – Utterson's first view of the route to Jekyll's cabinet)

 # Progress check

Use the chart below to review the skills you have developed in this chapter.
For each column, start at the bottom box and work your way up towards the highest level in the top box. Tick the box to show you have achieved that level.

Personal response	Textual references	Technical accuracy
I can sustain a critical response to *Jekyll and Hyde* and interpret the themes convincingly ☐	I can use well-integrated textual references from *Jekyll and Hyde* to support my interpretation ☐	I use a wide range of vocabulary and can spell and punctuate consistently accurately ☐
I can develop a coherent response to *Jekyll and Hyde* and explain the themes clearly ☐	I can use quotations and other textual references from *Jekyll and Hyde* to support my explanation ☐	I use a range of vocabulary and can spell and punctuate, mostly accurately ☐
I can make some comments on the themes in *Jekyll and Hyde* ☐	I can make references to some details from *Jekyll and Hyde* ☐	I use a simple range of vocabulary and spell and punctuate with some accuracy ☐

Writing about literary texts in exams

In an exam you will have to demonstrate your understanding of *The Strange Case of Dr Jekyll and Mr Hyde* in a limited time. There is no formula to follow to write the perfect essay and each essay will have its own strengths and weaknesses.

One essay may have a very strong introduction but fail to develop the points made, while another may use lots of textual knowledge but not create a coherent series of points showing personal understanding and engagement with the text.

You are more likely to write effective answers in exams if you avoid the common mistakes listed below, then try to follow the Things to do! advice.

Common mistakes

- ☒ Poor timing – too much time spent on another essay in the exam or on one particular point

- ☒ Not answering the actual question – trying to answer one you revised instead

- ☒ Limited personal engagement with the text and task resulting in narrative retelling of the plot

- ☒ Limited development of ideas – points are made but not explained

- ☒ Overuse of quotations – too many or long quotations can leave little room for expressing and developing personal ideas

- ☒ Underuse of quotations – not enough quotation means the points made lack evidence and are less convincing

- ☒ Overuse of technical and literary terms – knowing the terms but not linking the points made to the question or explaining the effect

Things to do!

- ☑ Revise appropriately so that you have the necessary knowledge about plot, character, themes, context and use of language.

- ☑ Be prepared to answer different types of question so that your knowledge is adaptable.

- ☑ Understand how to structure an answer so that your introduction is developed throughout and your conclusion sums up the important issues that you have raised.

- ☑ Use literary terms accurately and a sophisticated critical vocabulary when appropriate – especially when explaining the effects of language.

- ☑ Use short integrated quotations accurately to support the points you make.

- ☑ Maintain a consistent viewpoint throughout.

- ☑ Write in a clear and coherent style with technical accuracy.

Effective revision techniques

Any approach to revision has to be personal and one that works for you. Some people prefer rereading notes made in class, while others prefer to add new points or make new notes based on different learning. Whatever the approach you take, you must be prepared to give adequate time to prepare. Any notes you use for revision must work for you and help you to remember key points and ideas.

Plot and structure

Creating a revision page for each chapter of the novella allows you to summarize the key events from your own perspective. You could colour-code the characters who appear in each chapter to track the development of their role throughout the novella. Write three 'key things to remember' in bullet points at the end of each chapter. If you read the bullet points first when revising, this will be a quick reminder of events before going into more detail. Here is an example that could be used for Chapter 1:

Chapter 1 – Key Points

- The reader is introduced to Mr Utterson who seems quiet and reserved but meets Mr Enfield for weekly walks.

- Enfield tells Utterson of the day he dealt with a man called Hyde who had trampled a young girl and made him pay her family.

- We learn that Utterson is worried because he already knows the name of Hyde but does not discuss any more details with Enfield and they agree not to talk about it again.

Activity 1

a) Create a revision page for each chapter in the novella, like the one shown above.

b) Add a cover sheet with one key point from each chapter for even faster tracking.

It is important that you show knowledge of the whole text in your answers, whatever the specific subject identified in the question. Gaining an overview in this way helps you to 'see' the novella as a whole and makes it easier to select appropriate references and events.

One way of gaining an overview is by creating a series of graphic images to represent the narrative in each chapter. Place the images on one sheet of paper and draw arrows between them so that you can quickly and clearly see the chronological order.

For example, Chapter 3 could be represented like this:

Activity 2

Design your own graphical images for each chapter. You could add a key quotation or two to each image.

Character

Create a character page for each character in the novella. You can divide this into sections to suit you using a particular colour for each character. You could use the following headings in the structure:

- Main role in the plot
- Relationships with others
- Key quotations
- Key points to remember.

This approach can be adapted as you develop your learning over time. Make sure that you restrict the notes to one page for each character. As the exam approaches, this can be reduced to one flash-card for each character so that you can carry them with you more easily.

Activity 3

Design your own character pages for Jekyll and Hyde.

Activity 4

It can be very helpful to create charts to represent the relationships between the characters in the novella. You may wish to think about:

- how each of the characters relate to Jekyll or Hyde in the narrative as whole (remembering that Jekyll and Hyde are two sides of the same character) – see an example of how this could be done below
- drawing lines between the characters to represent links with thicker lines for stronger relationships
- writing key points – perhaps quotations – to show the links in the relationship along the line.

	Hyde	Jekyll
Utterson	Suspects he is trying to blackmail Jekyll	Respects him as an old friend although is worried for him
Enfield	Shocked by his behaviour at trampling the young girl	Knows of him as a respectable person
Poole	Worries he has murdered his master	Respects him as his long-time master
Lanyon	Shocked to discover he is the other side to Jekyll	An old friend with whom he has fallen out due to a scientific disagreement

Design your own version using whichever ideas you feel would help you.

Language

Upgrade

You will not be expected to structure a whole essay around the use of language in *The Strange Case of Dr Jekyll and Mr Hyde* in an exam question. However, you will only be able to access the highest marks by investigating some language use in your essay. For instance, you can explain the way that imagery is used in the novella to convey the intense feelings of characters and/or to introduce surprising developments in the plot and explore this point further with specific comments about the effect on the narrative (and/or characters) at these points.

Activity 5

Create records of examples of powerful imagery used for each character, place and key event. You decide what form the record should take – table, graph, chart, graphic images, etc. Remember: include the potential effect on a reader at a particular point in the novella.

You could make 'language' a separate part of your character notes so that language is seen as integral (essential) to that character. This will also help you to see that comments on language support questions on the presentation of themes and characters.

Themes

Themes can be revised in a similar way. Some examples are:

- Theme headings linked to characters. For instance, your page on 'Secrecy' as a theme may include one section that notes the number of secrets kept (or information withheld) by each character.
- An image representing the theme could be the centre of a spider diagram or chart that enables you to make links between events and characters.

Activity 6

Complete the spider diagram on the theme of 'Secrecy' that has been started below.

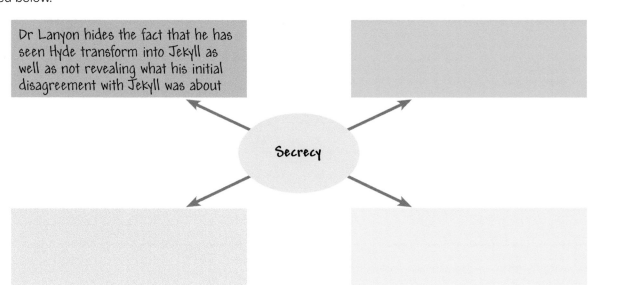

Dr Lanyon hides the fact that he has seen Hyde transform into Jekyll as well as not revealing what his initial disagreement with Jekyll was about

Secrecy

Answering questions in the exam

Appropriate language

Essays do not have to be written in a style that is extremely formal and academic in order to gain the highest marks. A clear and consistent style is needed so that you can effectively communicate to the examiner what you think about appropriate aspects of the novella. Don't worry about crossings-out – the examiner will only assess the parts you indicate as your final answer.

Activity 7

You should avoid writing that Stevenson 'says' or 'speaks about' something or someone in an essay. The use of these verbs in this context is too informal.

Look at the following list of verbs that can be used appropriately to describe what a writer 'does' in a text. You could also use these verbs to describe the effect of characters, a word, phrase or sentence.

describes	argues (that)	thinks (that)	portrays (pictures)	dramatizes
emphasizes	allows (us)	pictures	knows (that)	depicts	creates
makes (us)	illustrates	reflects	stages	demonstrates (that)	recounts
shocks	pleases (us)	focuses (upon)	states	juxtaposes	examines
analyses	encourages (us to)	implies (that)	senses (that)	warns (us that)
asks/answers	succeeds (by/in…)	shows	understands	conveys (an idea)	pities

Notice that:

- all the verbs are in the present tense (because discussing the text is always in the moment)
- the 'us' refers to the reader in the context of the novella – never the 'audience', as this word is directly linked to dramatic performances and the theatre.

a) Which verbs would you use to describe the use of imagery?

----

b) Which verbs relate to arguing a point?

----

c) Which verbs relate to emotion?

----

d) See how many other verbs you can add to the list.

When using **conjunctions** in your essays to develop points, be careful of sounding too formulaic, as this gives the impression of being too pre-planned. You should use conjunctions in a flexible way so that their use is natural for your style and appropriate for the tone of the essay. Avoid using 'firstly… secondly… thirdly…' if possible.

> **conjunction** a word used to connect clauses or sentences (sometimes referred to as a 'connective' word)

Activity 8

Look at the following list of more formal conjunctions that can be appropriately used in your essays. Where there is an informal version of the word, this is placed in brackets to remind you of the alternative.

| however (but) | furthermore (also) | additionally (also) | therefore (so) |

| nevertheless / nonetheless (anyway) | initially (firstly) | whereas | similarly |

| for example (e.g.) | for instance (e.g.) | in conclusion |

| in other words / that is (i.e.) | ultimately (finally) | consequently | alternatively |

| although | notwithstanding (even knowing that) | on the other hand |

Most of these words or phrases can be used at the beginning of or within sentences. Practise using them and develop your style so that you are comfortable with them.

The following student response discusses Utterson's loyalty to Henry Jekyll. Replace the highlighted words with the most appropriate more formal conjunctions.

> Utterson is a loyal friend to Henry Jekyll throughout the novella, but he does have more and more doubts as the novella develops. We firstly see his worries in Chapter 2 where he is concerned that Jekyll has named Edward Hyde as the sole beneficiary of his will. Even so, as a professional lawyer, he has to accept the wishes of his friend, even though he may not approve. Also, his visit to Dr Lanyon and the way he clearly disagrees with Jekyll's ideas add to Utterson's concern that his friend is suffering in some way. So, it is no surprise that Utterson agrees (though with an 'irrepressible sigh') to abide by his friend's wishes and help Edward Hyde in the event of Jekyll's death or disappearance.

Informal	More formal
But	
Firstly	
Even so	
Also	
So	

Planning answers

You do not have time to plan an answer in detail in the exam. Your revision strategies, if effective, should have prepared you to be able to think quickly and to select appropriate ideas and quotations. However, a brief plan, taking one or two minutes, can help to organize your thinking. In this plan you should jot down ideas for an introduction, followed by main points and a conclusion.

Look at this brief plan for an essay asking how Stevenson presents Dr Jekyll in the novella.

> **Introduction:** eponymous character, whose genius and weakness drives the narrative

> **Section 1:** discuss his struggle with the results of his work and the way Dr Lanyon reacts to his research and his horror at the result

> **Section 2:** discuss his relationship with Utterson and how the lawyer portrays his friend before he knows the truth

> **Section 3:** discuss the fact that Jekyll remains aware of being Hyde and enjoys what he does – he becomes Hyde for selfish reasons until he loses control

> **Conclusion:** summarize the points discussed and focus on the 'religious' and moral argument over 'good' and 'evil' in the way Stevenson presents the character of Henry Jekyll in the text

Remember:

- A plan like this cannot remind you of *all* the detail.
- You can write more than one paragraph within a 'section'.
- You do not have to follow it exactly – you can change your mind.

Activity 9

Create a quick plan for an essay asking you to discuss the presentation of Dr Lanyon in the novella. Think about what Stevenson does and the methods he uses.

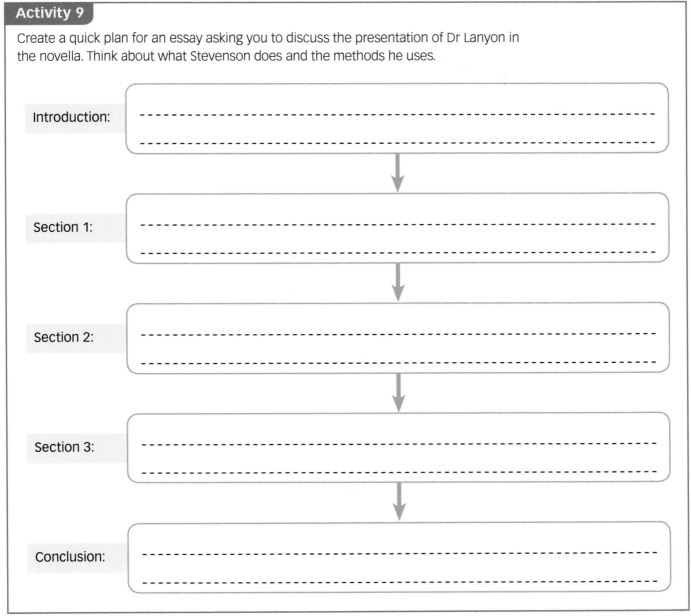

Introduction:

Section 1:

Section 2:

Section 3:

Conclusion:

Effective introductions

An introduction allows the examiner to see the range of points you intend to discuss. The subjects you raise and the knowledge you show, even if briefly, should demonstrate that you can handle the material confidently and have a strong overview and grasp of the text.

You should:

- show that you have clearly understood the question
- summarize the points you will be looking at in more detail later in the essay
- demonstrate an overview by referring to points throughout the text
- end by linking in to the subject of the next paragraph.

Look at the following sample exam question:

Read the following extract from Chapter 2. In it Mr Utterson has just met Mr Hyde for the first time.

'Poor Harry Jekyll,' he thought, 'my mind misgives me he is in deep waters! He was wild when he was young; a long while ago to be sure; but in the law of God, there is no statute of limitations. Ay, it must be that; the ghost of some old sin, the cancer of some concealed disgrace: punishment coming, *pede claudo*, years after memory has forgotten and self-love condoned the fault.' And the lawyer, scared by the thought, brooded awhile on his own past, groping in all the corners of memory, lest by chance some Jack-in-the-Box of an old iniquity should leap to light there. His past was fairly blameless; few men could read the rolls of their life with less apprehension; yet he was humbled to the dust by the many ill things he had done, and raised up again into a sober and fearful gratitude by the many that he had come so near to doing, yet avoided. And then by a return on his former subject, he conceived a spark of hope. 'This Master Hyde, if he were studied,' thought he, 'must have secrets of his own: black secrets, by the look of him; secrets compared to which poor Jekyll's worst would be like sunshine. Things cannot continue as they are. It turns me cold to think of this creature stealing like a thief to Harry's bedside; poor Harry, what a wakening! And the danger of it; for if this Hyde suspects the existence of the will, he may grow impatient to inherit. Ay, I must put my shoulder to the wheel – if Jekyll will but let me,' he added, 'if Jekyll will only let me.' For once more he saw before his mind's eye, as clear as a transparency, the strange clauses of the will. *(Chapter 2)*

Starting with this extract, how does Stevenson present the relationship between Dr Jekyll and Mr Utterson? Write about:

- how Stevenson presents Mr Utterson in this extract
- how Stevenson presents the friendship and loyalty towards Dr Jekyll shown by Mr Utterson in the novella as a whole.

The following are examples of introductions to essays attempting to answer this question.

Introduction 1

Brief overview of the extract.

Placing the extract in context.

Integrated quotation from the extract.

Integrated quotation from elsewhere in the text.

Some focus on the question.

Integrated quotation from the extract.

Short link to the rest of the essay.

> In this extract, taken from the end of Chapter 2, Mr Utterson, who is a lawyer and a friend of Dr Jekyll, is showing what he thinks about the situation with Mr Hyde. He has just talked to the 'pale and dwarfish' man. He describes him as a having a 'displeasing smile' and already knows what he has done to the young girl he 'trampled' from the story told to him by Mr Enfield in Chapter 1. Utterson is not comfortable after his meeting with Hyde; he calls him 'hardly human' and worries about what Hyde knows about the past of Dr Jekyll to cause him to be mentioned in the will. Utterson is determined to help his friend and this is shown by the way 'poor Harry' is repeated. I am now going to look at the extract in more detail and the power of their friendship in the novel.

Things to improve:

- More comment is needed on the relationship with Jekyll in the rest of the novella.
- There could be more use of short quotations linked to Jekyll reflecting their relationship.
- Link more closely to the content of the next section of the essay.

Activity 10

Annotate the next introduction in the same way as the previous one to show the following:

- integrated quotations from the extract or elsewhere in the text
- links to the question
- context.

Introduction 2

> Mr Utterson is powerfully portrayed in this extract as a loyal and caring friend to Henry Jekyll. We have earlier been informed that his affections for long-time friends were 'like ivy' and he clearly feels that Jekyll is under the dangerous influence of a man with 'black secrets' and that he could be harmed by 'the ghost of some old sin'. The strength of his loyalty is shown in the extract by the way that Utterson is prepared to think better of his friend and to dismiss any thought of him doing anything particularly morally wrong. He is assuming that Hyde is blackmailing his friend, and in the rest of the novel he tries to save Jekyll from humiliation. At this point the reader is unaware of the true nature of Hyde's relationship with Jekyll and so we can admire Utterson's intentions as his friend. Utterson is the key to the reader discovering Jekyll's secret; it is his determination that leads him to the awful truth.

Things to improve:

- There could be more short integrated quotations to reflect the friendship between Utterson and Jekyll.
- There could be more reference to some of the detail of Utterson's role in the rest of the novel.
- Link more closely to the content of the next section.

Activity 11

Write an effective introduction to one of the
following questions on a separate piece of paper:

> Explore the presentation of secrets and lies in *The Strange Case of Dr Jekyll and Mr Hyde*.

> Examine the ways that the conflict between good and evil is presented in *The Strange Case of Dr Jekyll and Mr Hyde*.

> Explore the presentation of the minor characters in *The Strange Case of Dr Jekyll and Mr Hyde*.

Effective conclusions

The conclusion should draw the essay to a logical close.

You should:

- show that you have clearly answered the question
- summarize the key points you have made through the essay (though try not to repeat the same sentence structures and vocabulary if possible)
- demonstrate a reflective sense of overview
- use some short quotations to clearly support points
- end the essay with a clear and well-supported analysis.

Activity 12

a) Read the following conclusion to a student's essay that is answering the sample exam question on page 90. Look at the comments suggesting how it could have been improved.

Student 1

Left still desperately searching for a way to save his friend Jekyll at the
end of Chapter 8, Utterson is a man who is yet to learn the truth but
holds it in his hand in the shape of Jekyll's final letter. After all that
Utterson has done to try and protect the public name of Dr Jekyll, it
has been thrown back in his face and he is left to face the shame. We
can only agree with Jekyll himself when he ends his cover note with:
'Your unworthy and unhappy friend, HENRY JEKYLL'.

More of an overview comment needed here.

More about what the truth is and how it was 'predicted' in the extract from Chapter 2?

Include a reference to an example of this.

An unexplained assertion – could be argued but needs development.

A valid point made but some more examples of why he was 'unworthy' would support this comment.

b) Now read the second student example. Note the positive aspects and make notes
on where and how you think it could be improved.

Student 2

In conclusion, Stevenson clearly portrays the loyalty felt by Utterson to Jekyll at the point of the novel from which the extract is taken (Chapter 2). The extract depicts the early stages of anxiety felt by Utterson for his friend, 'poor Harry'. By the end of Chapter 8, as he stands over the lifeless form of Edward Hyde (the 'self-destroyer'), Utterson is poised to learn the full truth, though he suspects a 'dire catastrophe'. Even at this point, where it is clear to the reader that he can help Jekyll no more, he is still striving to defend the reputation of his friend, convincing Poole that 'we may at least save some credit'. By the end of the novella the reader can only feel sympathy for both Jekyll, whose life has been lost to scientific research, and Utterson, whose friendship and loyalty has been tested to destruction.

---

c) Write your own conclusion to the same question. Try to avoid the weaknesses of
the examples and leave the examiner feeling that you have a confident grasp of
the text and can offer valid and well-supported points.

Progress check

Use the chart below to review the skills you have developed in this chapter. For each column, start at the bottom box and work your way up towards the highest level in the top box. Tick the box to show you have achieved that level.

I can sustain a critical response to *Jekyll and Hyde* and interpret the context convincingly ☐	I can analyse the effects of Stevenson's use of language, structure and form in *Jekyll and Hyde*, using subject terms judiciously ☐	I can use well-integrated textual references from *Jekyll and Hyde* to support my interpretation ☐
I can develop a coherent response to *Jekyll and Hyde* and explain the context clearly ☐	I can explain how Stevenson uses language, structure and form to create effects in *Jekyll and Hyde*, using relevant subject terms ☐	I can use quotations and other textual references from *Jekyll and Hyde* to support my explanation ☐
I can make some comments on the context in *Jekyll and Hyde* ☐	I can identify some of Stevenson's methods in *Jekyll and Hyde* and use some subject terms ☐	I can make references to some details from *Jekyll and Hyde* ☐
Personal response	**Language, structure, form**	**Textual references**

Glossary

alter ego a second self inside, different from an individual's normal personality

Calvinist a member of a major branch of the Protestant religion that follows the teaching of John Calvin; Stevenson was brought up in a Calvinist family

colonialism the practice by in which an empire rules colonies, to benefit from their resources

conjunction a word used to connect clauses or sentences (sometimes referred to as a 'connective' word)

conservative an attitude towards life that dislikes change and respects tradition

context the situation or circumstances in which a text is written, published or read

dialogue conversation in a book, play or film

eponymous refers to the character's name forming part of the title of the novel

evocative creating strong images and/or feelings

gothic fiction a literary style characterized by tales of horror and the supernatural

hierarchy a system of ranking according to birth, status and authority, etc.

honourable having the respect of others due to previous reputation and behaviour

internal monologue a literary device where a character's thoughts are presented as speech

juxtaposition one thing put next to another for contrast

metaphor a figure of speech applied to something to suggest a resemblance without using the words 'like' or 'as'

metonymy the substitution of the name of an attribute for that of the thing meant, for example 'crown' for 'power' or 'authority' in a country

novella a prose text that is longer than a short story but shorter than a standard novel

personification when human qualities are given to something non-human, such as an object or idea

plot the sequence of events in a narrative

protagonist a main character

psyche the human mind and spirit – from a religious perspective

psychology the scientific study of the mind and how it influences behaviour

science fiction fiction that uses ideas about scientific discovery to imagine a future that is often frightening

scripture religious text used in church, home and school

Sigmund Freud an influential figure in the early days of the study of the mind; he was particularly interested in deep motivations that we may not even be aware of

simile a figure of speech applied to something to suggest a resemblance, introduced by the words 'like' or 'as'

structure how a text is organized, overall and in all aspects

Victorian compromise the ability of middle- and upper-class Victorian society to indulge their wilder desires but maintain their outwardly respectable appearance

OXFORD
UNIVERSITY PRESS

Great Clarendon Street, Oxford, OX2 6DP, United Kingdom

Oxford University Press is a department of the University of Oxford.
It furthers the University's objective of excellence in research, scholarship,
and education by publishing worldwide. Oxford is a registered trade mark
of Oxford University Press in the UK and in certain other countries

© Oxford University Press 2017

First published in 2017

British Library Cataloguing in Publication Data

Data available

ISBN 978-019-839885-1

10 9 8 7 6 5 4 3 2

Printed in Great Britain by CPI Group (UK) Ltd., Croydon CR0 4YY

Acknowledgements

We have made every effort to contact copyright holders of third party
material before publication. If notified, we will rectify any omissions at
the earliest opportunity.

The publisher and authors would like to thank the following for
permission to use photographs and other copyright material:

Cover: Three Lions/Getty Images

Artwork by Oxford University Press